Power and Grace

Power and Grace

A Theology of the Psalms

MARK J. MANGANO

WIPF & STOCK · Eugene, Oregon

POWER AND GRACE
A Theology of the Psalms

Copyright © 2011 Mark J. Mangano. All rights reserved. Except for brief quotations in critical publications or reviews, no part of this book may be reproduced in any manner without prior written permission from the publisher. Write: Permissions, Wipf and Stock Publishers, 199 W. 8th Ave., Suite 3, Eugene, OR 97401.

All scripture quotations, unless otherwise indicated, are taken from the Holy Bible, New International Version®, NIV®. Copyright ©1973, 1978, 1984 by Biblica, Inc.™ Used by permission of Zondervan. All rights reserved worldwide. www.zondervan.com.

Revised Standard Version of the Bible, copyright © 1952 [2nd edition, 1971] by the Division of Christian Education of the National Council of the Churches of Christ in the United States of America. Used by permission. All rights reserved.

Wipf & Stock
An Imprint of Wipf and Stock Publishers
199 W. 8th Ave., Suite 3
Eugene, OR 97401

www. wipfandstock.com

ISBN 13: 978-1-60899-909-5

Manufactured in the U.S.A.

*Thanks be to God for a lifetime of close friends—
Brent, Mark, Bill, Ron, Russ, Chris, Brian, Jeff, and Fred.*

Contents

Preface / ix

1. Introduction / 1
2. The Names of God / 8
3. God Is Awesome / 17
4. God Is Creator / 24
5. God Is King / 33
6. God Is Refuge / 47
7. God is Deliverer / 58
8. God Is Great, Good, and Loving / 68
9. God Is Righteous / 76
10. God Is Shepherd / 84
11. God Is Present / 92
12. The House of the LORD / 103
13. The Praise of God / 111

Bibliography / 123
Scripture Index / 125

Preface

THEOLOGIANS ARE SCIENTISTS. We collect data from the world around, from life experiences, from the testimony of witnesses, and from sacred texts. Once catalogued and synthesized, these pieces of data inform our thinking about God, our hypothesis, if you will. It is very difficult work, plagued at any moment by misperception, bias, and faulty thinking.

A scientist may be passionate about science, but must remain dispassionate in working out the scientific method. A theologian must always exercise caution in speaking of the deity, but must love him with all of her thoughts, passions, and actions. This is a consuming love, a love that knows both risk and reward.

Though intellectual pursuit of God is important, he typically eludes the grasp of our inquiry and transcends our hypotheses. We affirm that he created and redeemed us, but who can comprehend how awesome is his power and vast his grace? He is the one we desire, love, and in whom we hope, yet we often feel abandoned and adrift.

Every book in the Bible must be studied for its contribution to our understanding of and love for God. On the pages which follow, I explore with you theological truths from the Psalms. These truths will inform our thoughts about God and arouse our passions for him. These studies will crescendo in meditation, prayer, and song.

I applaud the efforts of Lori Thomas in editing these pages. Her suggestions were greatly appreciated. I alone am responsible for any remaining mistakes. I also applaud the technological savvy of Philip Draughan and JJ Simpson. Their genius saved me countless times! Even though most of this work was completed during a sabbatical, I thank my family for enduring the journey. Finally, thanks be to God for his Word, especially the book of Psalms!

1

Introduction

For the person of faith, God is present from birth to old age. This truth is affirmed in the Psalms. Psalm 71:6 speaks of God's presence at birth: "From birth I have relied on you; *you brought me forth from my mother's womb.*" The italicized portion of the quotation is literally, "From the innermost parts of my mother you were the one cutting me loose." The psalmist portrays God as a midwife cutting the umbilical cord (see also 22:9). The same psalmist sees his old age as an opportunity to tell of God's power and might to the next generation (71:18).

The psalmists affirm that God's presence actually predates birth and extends beyond the grave. Psalm 139:13 affirms the former, "For you created my inmost being; you knit me together in my mother's womb," while Psalm 71:20 hints at the latter, "Though you have made me see troubles, many and bitter, you will restore my life again; from the depths of the earth you will again bring me up" (see also 73:24).

Through the course of our lives lived in the presence of God we encounter his power and grace. "One thing God has spoken, two things have I heard; that you, O God, are strong, and that you, O Lord, are loving" (62:11–12a).

Power and grace! Thus the name of the book you now hold in your hands. The purpose of this little volume is to explore the dimensions of God's power and grace. How awesome is his power? How vast is his grace?

Each step into our discovery begins with a study of the Book of Psalms, the Psalter (a "psalmbook"). This exploration is also a journey into our hearts, from which, I hope and pray, will burst forth meditation, song, and prayer.

Why this combination of study, meditation, song, and prayer? Since God has chosen to reveal himself (Ps 98:2), he expects to be known.

A vital dimension of our knowing God is a *study* of His Word. In our *meditation* upon the Psalms, the Holy Spirit opens our minds and hearts that "we may understand what God has freely given us" (1 Cor 2:12). *Song* and *prayer* are fitting responses to his gift. Praise and prayer are the characteristic modes of a life of faith.

The Psalms themselves are sung prayers or prayed singing. The very nature of the content, the center, and object of the Psalms calls for praise and prayer.

Only four times in the Psalms do we encounter the verb "to pray" (5:2; 32:6; 72:15; 106:30; GK 7137). The noun form, "prayer" (GK 9525), is much more common, though, appearing thirty-two times, five of these in the psalm "titles" (or "superscriptions") (17:1; 86:1; 90:1; 102:1; 142:1). The psalmists urgently plead (using the command form of the verb, the imperative) with God to hear their prayers (4:1; 39:12; 54:2; 84:8; 102:1; 143:1), or to give ear to their prayers (17:1; 55:1; 86:6), or to listen to them (61:1).

The verb "hear" (GK 9048) occurs seventy-nine times. Thirty-nine times God is the subject of the verb. Fifteen times an imperative is used: "Hear, O LORD!" (30:10). He is "commanded" to hear "my prayer" (see the references above); "my voice" (27:7; 119:149; 130:2); "my cry" (28:2; 61:1); "my plea" (17:1); "my word" (17:6; the NIV renders this word "prayer"); and once "me" (64:1). Twice the LORD uses the imperative upon his people (50:7; 81:8).

The noun "song" (GK 8877) occurs forty-two times, thirty of these in the psalm "superscriptions" (for example, Pss 120 to 134). Listen to Ps 28:7: "The LORD is my strength and my shield; my heart trusts in him, and I am helped. My heart leaps for joy and I will give thanks to him in song."

The verb "sing" (GK 8876) occurs twenty-seven times. Psalm 89:1 reads, "I will sing of the LORD's great love forever." Six times the noun "song" and the verb "sing" are paired, that is, "sing a song" (33:3; 96:1; 98:1; 137:4; 144:9; 149:1).

Celebration in song and community go together; they are dependent upon each other. Without the celebration of praise, a community has no real center. A church gathering without praise is illogical (and, I hope, unheard of). Psalm 68 narrates a joyous celebration of God's presence amidst his people. Notice how celebration is impossible without community and community without celebration. "Your procession has come into view, O God, the procession of my God and king into the sanctuary. In front are the singers, after them the musicians; with them are the maidens playing tambourines. Praise God in the great congregation; praise the LORD in the assembly of Israel" (68:24–26).

A second verb, "to make music in praise of God" (GK 2376), occurs forty-one times. In one verse alone, the verb is used four times: "Sing praises to God, sing praises; sing praises to our King, sing praises" (47:6; see also 66:4). This psalmist then uses the same verb in the very next verse! (Maybe I should censor my mind when I grow weary of repetition in today's praise!) Ten times these two verbs of praise occur together in the same verse (21:13; 27:6; 57:7; 68:4, 32; 101:1; 104:33; 105:2; 108:1; 144:9).

In the world of the Psalms, as is the case in our own lives, not all is praise and prayer. Questions of doubt are plentiful in the Psalter. Several Hebrew phrases are translated "How long?" (1) "Until when?" is the most frequent. "My soul is in anguish. How long, O LORD, how long? I am worn out from groaning; all night long I flood my bed with weeping and drench my couch with tears. My eyes grow weak with sorrow; they fail because of all my foes" (6:3, 6–7). See also 74:10; 80:4; 90:13; 94:3; 119:82, 84 (cf. 41:5; 42:2; 101:2 for a similar Hebrew construction). (2) "Until what?" occurs in four verses. "We are objects of reproach to our neighbors, of scorn and derision to those around us. How long, O LORD? Will you be angry forever?" (79:4–5a). "How long, O LORD? Will you hide yourself forever? How long will your wrath burn like fire?" (89:46). See also 4:2; 74:9. (3) "Until where?" occurs five times in three verses. "How long, O LORD? Will you forget me forever? How long will you hide your face from me? How long must I wrestle with my thoughts and every day have sorrow in my heart? How long will my enemy triumph over me?" (13:1–2). See also 62:3. (4) "Like what?" occurs in two verses. "How long must your servant wait? When will you punish my persecutors?" (119:84). "O Lord, how long will you look on? Rescue my life from their ravages, my precious life from these lions" (35:17).

At Psalm 10:1 two similar questions are voiced. The first one: "Why, O LORD, do you stand far off?" The adjective "distant, far" occurs seven times, but only twice in a question. The second occurrence is more familiar to the reader. "My God, my God, why have you forsaken me? Why are you so far from saving me?" (22:1). The second question: "Why do you hide yourself in times of trouble?" This verb "hide, conceal"

(GK 6623) appears only four times in the Psalms, and only this one time in a question (see also 55:1).

The verb "reject" (GK 2396) is used ten times in the Psalter. It is used to express personal despair. "Why have you rejected me?" (43:2; 88:14; 89:38). It is also used to express the community's bewilderment. "Why have you rejected us forever, O God? Why does your anger smolder against the sheep of your pasture?" (74:1; see also 44:9, 23; 60:1, 10; 77:7; 108:11).

In the Psalms, then, we have the worst of times (119:123) and the best of times. We have life! "Weeping may remain for a night, but rejoicing comes in the morning" (30:5b). "You [God] turned my wailing into dancing; you removed my sackcloth and clothed me with joy" (30:11). Psalm 42:5 asks, "Why are you downcast, O my soul? Why so disturbed within me?" Three verses later the psalmist says, "By day the LORD directs his love, at night his song is with me—a prayer to *the God of my life*" (42:8).

When David was in the Judean wilderness, a fugitive in Saul's Israel, he spoke metaphorically of his desert prison as a "dry and weary land where there is no water" (Ps 63:1c). The worst of times to be sure! And yet, David says, "Because your love is better than life, my lips will glorify you. I will praise you as long as I live, and in your name I will lift up my hands" (63:3–4). The best of times indeed!

In the Psalms we can go from the worst of times to the best of times. What accounts for these "mood swings?" What can explain the movement from lament to praise? One possibility is that God has answered the psalmist's prayers. God's answer to prayer may be "heard" when a word or thought is impressed on the believer's heart, or when the presence of the Lord becomes real for the anguished soul, or when the believer receives some sign of God's favor (74:9; 86:17). Whenever God answers prayer, he shows he has not forsaken the troubled soul. A second possibility is a change in circumstances. If I am distraught over the circumstances in my life, and then those circumstances change, praise or thanksgiving would naturally flow from my heart.

Each chapter in this book will begin with study. God is our teacher; we are his students! The book of Psalms is our book; the Holy Spirit our guide.

When you cast a stone into a lake, eventually the ripples that stone created will merge with the shoreline. The Psalms are like that stone, casting forth currents throughout the rest of Scripture, eventually coming ashore (for the Christian) in the New Testament. When I note a New Testament connection to or parallel with the Psalms, I will mark it with the heading "New Testament Parallel."

In each study, I will pose a question or questions that require meditation. These questions are meant to bring an added dimension to our study, translating the truth of scripture for our head, heart, and hands—our thoughts, passions, and actions. I will mark these questions with the heading "Meditation."

The Psalms have inspired generations of songwriters. Many of the "blasts from the past" (hymns) and our "new songs" (which do not stay new for very long) reflect the lyrics of the Psalter. When we allow music to guide our thoughts and passions, I will mark this with the heading "Musical Reflection."

Each chapter will conclude with a printed prayer, and hopefully, your own spontaneous expressions of petition and praise. This will be marked with the heading "Prayer."

For the person who wants to do additional study of the key words mentioned in these chapters, I have also included the Edward W. Goodrick/John R. Kohlenberger III numbers (GK). These are the numbers assigned to the various Hebrew, Aramaic, and Greek words that comprise our Bibles by these two men in their *Zondervan NIV Exhaustive Concordance* (2nd edition). I have used the New International Version of the Holy Bible throughout these pages, except in chapters nine through eleven, where the Revised Standard Version is used.

Since this is a study in Psalms, don't expect to find your favorite gospel story. You may find reference to it, but don't expect it. Furthermore, I follow where the Psalms lead. If an idea is not found in the psalms, you will not find it here. Thus, my presentations here from Psalms will not be as well-rounded or developed as a full-Bible, Bible study.

In the Song of Songs we meet two lovers. The man is handsome (1:16); the woman is beautiful (7:6). These two English adjectives—handsome and beautiful—are excellent translations of a singular Hebrew word (keeping in mind, of course, the small difference grammatically between masculine and feminine). The man is charming (1:16); the woman is pleasing (7:6). These two adjectives are also excellent translations of a single Hebrew word group, a group used sparingly in the Psalms (only nine times). In the Song of Songs words are used to describe the physical beauty of two lovers—"handsome," "beautiful," "charming," and "pleasing." One of those words (the "charming/pleasing" word group) is used in the Psalms for the beauty of the LORD (27:4; 90:17), the beauty of his name (135:3; "pleasant" in the NIV), and the beauty of our worship (147:1; again "pleasant" in NIV).

Lovers yearn to know and to be known. Lovers are captivated by the presence of the beloved. Lovers are effusive in their praise of each other. Since God loves us, and we love him, then we yearn for his presence, take pleasure in knowing him (139:17), and delight in praising him!

In this book we shall praise God for his power and his grace. Chapters two through five will develop his power in the Psalms. Chapters six through thirteen focus on his grace.

Chapter 2: The Names of God	Chapter 6: God Is Refuge
Chapter 3: God Is Awesome	Chapter 7: God Is Deliverer
Chapter 4: God Is Creator	Chapter 8: God Is Great, Good, and Loving
Chapter 5: God Is King	Chapter 9: God Is Righteous
	Chapter 10: God Is Shepherd
	Chapter 11: God Is Present
	Chapter 12: The House of the LORD
	Chapter 13: The Praise of God

How was the Psalter put together? The book of Psalms is really five books in one. As you leaf through your copy of Psalms, you see this. Book one begins with Psalm 1; book two with Psalm 42; book three with Psalm 73; book four with Psalm 90; and book five with Psalm 107. The concluding psalm in each book closes with a doxology, an expression of praise to God (41:13; 72:18–19; 89:52; 106:48; 150:6).

The Psalter in ancient Israel was ever expanding (see 72:20) then to keep pace with the ever changing context of Israel's history (from monarchy to exile to restoration) and with the theological reflection those changing contexts brought.

The praise that is offered in many of our churches today blends the hymns from the past with contemporary choruses. The lyrics of our worship are in change also. This must always be the case. Why? Old and young will always gather around the cross and worship our Lord and Savior. But musical expression varies from generation to generation, as our culture and history change. The church is the context where the praises of multiple generations and cultures may find a voice. The Psalter was the place where God's ancient people voiced their praises and petitions in ever changing contexts.

On occasion in this book, I will present evidence from the Psalms book-by-book (book one through book five). I will do this to draw out certain important considerations. It is now time to begin. Turn the page, please.

2

The Names of God

"All the nations you have made will come and worship before you, O Lord; they will bring glory to your name." (Psalm 86:9)

THE NOUN "NAME" (GK 9005) occurs 109 times in the Psalter.[1] All but nine relate to our theology. Each star has a name (147:4). Lands have names (49:11). The name of a nation may be blotted out (9:5) or remembered no more (83:4). The name of a person may perish (41:5) or be blotted out (109:13), but one may hope that a king's name endures forever (72:17). If one forgets the name of God (44:20), or takes up the name of another god to his or her lips (16:4), then we have a case of idolatry.

THE LORD

Now to the name (GK 3378). In English convention, as is evident in the NIV, our God's personal name is LORD (notice the capital letters). This is the noun that the King James Version of the Bible routinely rendered *Jehovah*. Many believe that if the name were to be pronounced, we would hear *Yahweh*. He officially revealed this name at Exodus 3:15. In the Psalms this personal name is used 695 times. An abbreviated form of the name, *Yah*, as in *Hallelu Yah*, is used forty-three times.

Twice in the Psalms his name is explicitly identified. "His name is the LORD" (68:4). "Let them know that you, whose name is the LORD—that you alone are the Most High over all the earth" (83:18).

In the Psalter his name is awesome (99:3; 111:9), eternal (135:13), glorious (72:19), good (52:9; 54:6), great (76:1; 99:3), holy (30:4; 33:21;

---

1. A second noun (GK 2352) is twice translated *name* (30:4; 97:12) and twice *renown* (102:12; 135:13). His name is holy and his renown endures through all generations.

97:12; 103:1; 105:3; 106:47; 111:9; 145:21), majestic (8:1, 9), and near (75:1).

We may call on the name of the LORD (79:6; 80:18; 99:6; 105:1; 116:4, 13, 17). We may come in (118:26) and bless others through the name of the LORD (129:8). We may declare his name (22:22; 102:21). We may exalt his name (34:3). We may fear his name (61:5; 86:11; 102:15). We may give thanks to his name (106:47). We may glorify his name (29:2; 86:9, 12; 96:8; 105:3; 115:1). We may hope in his name (52:9). We may know and acknowledge his name (9:10; 91:14). We may lift up hands in praise of his name (63:4). We may love his name (5:11; 69:36; 119:132). We may make music to his name (92:1). We may perpetuate and remember his name (45:17; 119:55). We may praise his name (44:8; 48:10; 54:6; 69:30; 74:21; 96:2; 100:4; 103:1; 113:1, 2, 3; 122:4; 135:1; 138:2; 140:13; 142:7; 145: 1, 2, 21; 148:5, 13; 149:3). We may rejoice in his name (89:16). Some may revile his name (74:10, 18). We may seek his name (83:16). Mountain ranges sing for joy at his name (89:12). We may sing praises to his name (7:17; 9:2; 18:49; 61:8; 66:2, 4; 68:4; 135:3). We may trust in his name (20:7; 33:21).

We are saved (54:1) and protected from (20:1) our enemies by the name of God. In fact, through the name of the LORD, we trample our foes (44:5) and cut them off (118:10, 11, 12). "We will shout for joy when you [the king of Israel/Judah] are victorious and will lift up banners in the name of our God" (20:5; see also 89:24). Victory comes because "our help is in the name of the LORD, the Maker of heaven and earth" (124:8).

For the sake of his name, he guides (23:3; 31:3), forgives (25:11; 79:9), delivers (79:9), saves (106:8), shows love and compassion (109:21), and preserves life (143:11).

GOD

In the Psalms the LORD is called *Elohim* (GK 466) 365 times in 325 verses, *Eloah* (GK 468) four times in four verses (18:31; 50:22; 114:7; 139:19), and *El* (GK 446) seventy-six times in seventy-two verses. We routinely translate these words "God." These words suggest the power of deity.

Psalms 42–83 are referred to as the "Elohistic Psalter" because *Elohim* and *El* are commonly used. Outside this group, the noun LORD is by far the most common designation for deity. Of the 325 verses where

Elohim is used, 209 are found in the Elohistic Psalter (64 percent). Of the seventy-two verses where *El* is used, thirty-two are found in the Elohistic Psalter (44 percent).

GOD OF JACOB

The name "Jacob" appears thirty-four times in the Psalter. Twenty times the noun is synonymous with the nation of Israel (14:7; 22:23; 44:4; 47:4; 53:6; 59:13; 77:15; 78:5, 21, 71; 79:7; 85:1; 87:2; 99:4; 105:6, 10, 23; 114:1; 135:4; 147:19). This is understandable. In Genesis 32:28 Jacob is renamed Israel! What is surprising, though, is that there is no reference to the life and times of the patriarch Jacob.

The phrase "God of Jacob" appears twelve times in the Psalter (only six times elsewhere in the entire Old Testament: Exod 3:6, 15; 4:5; 2 Sam 23:1; Isa 2:3; Mic 4:2). A related expression, "The Mighty One of Jacob," is used twice: Ps 132:2, 5 (see also Gen 49:24; Isa 49:26; 60:16).

In the expression "God of Jacob," the "Jacob" component does not focus on the patriarch, but rather on "Israel." Of course, the LORD is the God of Jacob, that is, the God of Israel.

These twelve occurrences cluster around certain key ideas. (1) God protects: "May the name of the God of Jacob protect you" (20:1); "The God of Jacob is our fortress" (46:7, 11); "Blessed is he whose help is the God of Jacob" (146:5); "Sing for joy to God our strength, shout aloud to the God of Jacob" (81:1; see also v. 4); (2) God blesses (24:6; 84:8); and (3) God judges/rebukes (75:9; 76:6; 94:7; 114:7).

Seven times the LORD is actually called the "God of Israel" (41:13; 59:5; 68:8, 35; 69:6; 72:18; 106:48).

The Psalms mention Abraham four times. He is twice referred to as "servant" (105:6, 42). The covenant the LORD made with him is recalled to mind (105:9; see Gen 17:2; 22:16–18), as is the promise (105:42; see Gen 15:13–16). Only once is mention made of the "God of Abraham" (47:9). This psalm envisions "the nobles of the nations," "the kings of the earth," being called "the people of the God of Abraham." The psalmist here sees the fulfillment of the Abrahamic promise of Gen 12:3: "all peoples on earth will be blessed through you."[2]

---

2. "The Psalms are witness to the reality of Israel, even there where individual voices are raised. Israel is Yahweh's first partner, a people chosen, caught up in and enclosed in community and in faithfulness to the covenant. It is the first answer, the first witness. None other than the God of this people is the king of all peoples. The 'meaning' of Israel's existence is the mission to the peoples" (Kraus, *Theology of the Psalms*, 59).

Isaac is mentioned just once in the Psalms (105:9). He is coupled with his father, Abraham, and his son, Jacob, in remembering the LORD's covenant with the patriarchs. "He [the LORD] remembers his covenant forever, the word he commanded, for a thousand generations, the covenant he made with Abraham, the oath he swore to Isaac. He confirmed it to Jacob as a decree, to Israel as an everlasting covenant" (105:8–10).

THE HOLY ONE OF ISRAEL

Three times in the Psalms the LORD is called "The Holy One of Israel." (This title appears elsewhere in 2 Kgs 19:22, twenty-five times in Isaiah, and at Jer 50:29; 51:5; see also Ezek 39:7.) The "Holy One" is the "One-of-a-Kind One," the "Unique One." At 71:22 the psalmist praises the "Holy One of Israel" because his "faithfulness" is beyond compare. At 78:41–42 the power of the "Holy One of Israel" is unparalleled. At 89:18 the covenant relationship the "Holy One of Israel" has with Israel and her king is unprecedented. The holiness of the LORD leaves us speechless, without words to describe his unapproachable otherness. Our metaphors and similes are at best impoverished attempts to decipher the uniqueness of our God. Addison Road's popular Christian song (2009), "What Do I Know of Holy?" says it well (see 22:3).

MOST HIGH

The epithet "Most High" (GK 6609) is used twenty-one times of the LORD (7:17; 9:2; 18:13; 21:7; 46:4; 47:2; 50:14; 57:2; 73:11; 77:10; 78:17, 35, 56; 82:6; 83:18; 87:5; 91:1, 9; 92:1; 97:9; 107:11). It is a title that suggests the exalted status of the LORD. He is exalted over all kings, lands, peoples, foreign gods, and pantheons. "How awesome is the LORD Most High, the great King over all the earth!" (47:2; see also 83:18). "For you, O LORD, are the Most High over all the earth; you are exalted far above all gods" (97:9).

The Most High exercises this authority from heaven (18:13). The earthly seat of his authority is, however, the sanctuary on Mount Zion (87:5; 46:4). It is this dual citizenship of the LORD that makes his transcendence and imminence possible, that is, his power and love. The nearness of the transcendent One (the Most High) is captured at 91:9–10: "If you make the Most High your dwelling—even the LORD, who is my refuge—then no harm will befall you, no disaster will come near your tent."

ALMIGHTY

The noun "Almighty" (GK 8724) occurs only twice in the Psalms (68:14; 91:1). The might of the Almighty is depicted at 68:14: "When the Almighty scattered the kings in the land, it was like snow fallen on Zalmon." Since no battle at Zalmon is attested in the Scriptures, the verse is probably metaphorical rather than historical. The name Zalmon connotes "dark" or "black."[3] This establishes a nice contrast with the color of snow. Whenever the Almighty has been victorious in battle, his might has been as obvious as white on black, such as snow-capped peaks on a black mountain. And what is more obvious than a mountain to those who live in low lands or on the flats? The Scriptures are replete with examples of the Almighty scattering kings like snow on the battlefields.

LORD

The noun "Lord" (GK 123) appears fifty-seven times in the Psalms. Seven times LORD and Lord are conjoined (68:20; 71:5, 16; 73:28; 109:21; 140:7; 141:8), resulting in the translation "O Sovereign LORD." Once the expression "Lord of lords" is used (136:3). "As *adon* the God of Israel is the Lord and master in unlimited sovereignty and freedom."[4] David says of Yahweh, "You are my Lord" (16:2; 35:23), "our Lord" (8:1, 9). The Lord is the LORD Almighty (69:6).

The Lord is loving (62:12; 89:49), forgiving (130:3), good (86:5), and greater than all gods (135:5; 89:8). "You, O Lord, are a compassionate and gracious God, slow to anger, abounding in love and faithfulness" (86:15). He "daily bears our burdens" (68:19).

He scoffs at (2:4), laughs at (37:13), crushes (110:5), confuses (55:9), and brings down (59:11) the kings/wicked of the earth. When the Lord awakes, he beats back his enemies (78:65; 44:23; 79:12). David praises the Lord among the nations (57:9; 51:15; 68:32; 86:9, 12). Future generations will be told about him (22:30).

David cried to the Lord for mercy (30:8; 86:3; 130:2), for help (38:22; 77:2), and for rescue (35:17), knowing he would listen (66:18), answer (38:15), and sustain (54:4). David's longings lie open before the Lord (38:9). The Lord is our hope (39:7), help (40:17), and dwelling place (90:1). "Do not be far from me, O Lord" (35:22).

---

3. Tate, *Psalms 51–100*, 180.
4. Kraus, 30.

The following three words are not names of God per se, but these adjectives can easily be turned into names, the "Majestic One," the "Glorious One," and the "Living One."

The adjective "majestic" (GK 129) occurs just seven times in the Psalter. The term is used once for kings (136:18) and once for God's saints (16:3). The other five times the LORD is in mind. His name is majestic (8:1, 9); he is more majestic than mountains rich with game (76:4), and mightier than the thunder of the great waters (93:4).

The noun "beauty, glory, splendor" (GK 9514) occurs four times in the Psalms (71:8; 78:61; 89:18; 96:6). "Splendor and majesty are before him" (96:6). The LORD's splendor is praiseworthy. "My mouth is filled with your praise, declaring your splendor all day long" (71:8).

Three times the adjective "living" (GK 2645) is used of God (18:46; 42:2; 84:2). The phrase "land of the living" occurs four times in the Psalms (27:13; 52:5; 116:9; 142:5). It refers to the present life as opposed to nonexistence in the grave. "For you, O LORD, have delivered my soul from death, my eyes from tears, my feet from stumbling, that I may walk before the LORD in the land of the living" (116:8–9; see also 56:13).

The noun "light" (GK 240) occurs nineteen times in the Psalter. It is also not technically a name for deity. But for Christians it is just one step from "light" to the "Light of the World" (John 8:12). The LORD is wrapped in light (104:2). The LORD created the great lights (136:7; see also 37:6; 148:3). The LORD is my light (27:1). His word is a light for my path (119:105). "In your light we see light" (36:9). The psalmist prays that light and truth would guide him to the temple (43:3). Blessed are those "who walk in the light of your presence, O LORD" (89:15; see also 49:19; 56:13; 139:11). "Light is shed upon the righteous and joy on the upright in heart" (97:11; 112:4). "Let the light of your face shine upon us" (4:6b; see also 38:10; 44:3). God guided his people "with the cloud by day and with light from the fire all night" (78:14).

MY PORTION

"The LORD/God is my portion" occurs three times (73:26; 119:57; 142:5; see also 16:5; GK 2750). Ever since God told the priests, who never received a tribal land allotment, "I am your share (portion) and your inheritance among the Israelites" (Numbers 18:20), every thoughtful Israelite has understood that God is our only real security, our only true inheritance. Dare I say, he is the Ground of our Being!

The term "possession, property, inheritance" (GK 5709) appears twenty-three times. Not surprisingly, the Promised Land as inheritance is a recurrent motif in the Psalter. For example, Psalm 105:11 says, "To you I will give the land of Canaan as the portion you will inherit" (see also 2:8; 16:6; 37:18; 47:4; 68:9; 78:55; 111:6; 135:12 [twice]; 136:21, 22).

What is surprising is that the LORD considers his people to be his inheritance! For example, Psalm 33:12 reads, "Blessed is the nation whose God is the LORD, the people he chose for his inheritance" (see also 28:9; 74:2; 78:62, 71; 79:1; 94:5, 14; 106:5, 40). "Sons are a heritage from the LORD, children a reward from him" (127:3).

This idea is also reflected in the word "treasured possession" (GK 6035), which occurs only once in the Psalter (135:4), but often elsewhere in the OT (Exod 19:5; Deut 7:6; 14:2; 26:18; Mal 3:17). Just as kings have treasures (1 Chr 29:3; Eccl 2:8), and undoubtedly a prized jewel, a one-of-a-kind piece, a masterwork, so does the LORD—His people! "For the LORD has chosen Jacob to be his own, Israel to be his treasured possession" (135:4; see Titus 2:14 and 1 Peter 2:9).

The divine title "Lord of Hosts" will be examined in Chapter Five.

NEW TESTAMENT PARALLEL

When Jesus called himself "the light of the world" (John 8:12; see also 9:5), the Jews were celebrating the Feast of Tabernacles (7:2). This is a festival of light, much like Hanukah. The lights symbolized the pillar of fire in the wilderness and the glory that filled the temple. Jesus thereby claims to be the very God whose presence marks salvation. He is the light *of the world*, a reference to Isaiah 42:6—"a light for the Gentiles."

Walking in darkness is metaphoric for stumbling (John 11:9) or death (contrast the "light of life" in John 8:12 [see also 1:4; 12:36]). If we trust Jesus, then we will neither stumble nor die, but have life everlasting.

Psalm 27:1-2 brings together these themes. "The LORD is my light and my salvation—whom shall I fear? The LORD is the stronghold of my life—of whom shall I be afraid? When evil men advance against me to devour my flesh, when my enemies and my foes attack me, they will stumble and fall."

The term "Almighty" (GK 4120) appears ten times in the New Testament: once in a quotation of 2 Sam 7:8, 14 (2 Cor 6:18) and nine times in Revelation (1:8; 4:8; 11:17; 15:3; 16:7, 14; 19:6, 15; 21:22). In

Revelation God's superiority over all things is closely tied to his existence: "who is, and who was, and who is to come, the Almighty" (1:8; 4:8; 11:17; see also 15:3). His superiority is also tied to just and victorious judgment (16:7, 14; 19:15) and rule (19:6; 21:22).

"If you busy yourself in Psalms, you emerge knowing God."[5] How does one busy oneself in a psalm or in a characteristic of God? You study, you meditate, you sing, and you pray.

MEDITATION

- Which attribute of the name (The LORD) carries special importance today? Why?
- What is unique about the LORD? In what ways is he holy?
- Do you see your church as a prized jewel?

MUSICAL REFLECTION

In 1779 Edward Perronet (1726–1792), English pastor, wrote the powerful hymn "All Hail the Power of Jesus' Name," commonly known as the "National Anthem of Christianity."

> All hail the pow'r of Jesus' name! Let angels prostrate fall; bring forth the royal diadem, and crown Him Lord of all!
>
> Ye chosen seed of Israel's race, ye ransomed from the fall, hail Him who saves you by His grace, and crown Him Lord of all!
>
> Let ev'ry kindred, ev'ry tribe, on this terrestrial ball, to Him all majesty ascribe, and crown Him Lord of all!
>
> O that with yonder sacred throng ye at His feet may fall! We'll join the everlasting song, and crown Him Lord of all!

---

5. Willard, *Divine Conspiracy*, 65.

PRAYER

O Lord, our Lord, how majestic you are. You are resplendent in light, all glorious, and yet you are my portion, and we are your inheritance. We are your people; you are our God.

We marvel at the power of your name. In your name we have found salvation and hope, an identity and a home, our fears are quieted and our profoundest longings satisfied.

You are the Living One who renews our lives through the precious and beautiful name of Jesus, the Holy Savior of the world.

You are exalted over all, and yet you have cast your eyes on our needs, heard our prayers, enveloped us in your gracious presence, and taken us to yourself. We exalt you. We praise you. We thank you. We marvel at your unlimited sovereignty and freedom. Yet, your love and compassion bind you to us. You are our God, our Lord, our Help, our Light, our One-of-a-Kind God. We love you. We serve you. For the sake of your name, guide us, forgive us, deliver us, and save us. May your name be praised in heaven above and on earth below. Amen and Amen.

∽

What are your song and your prayer?

3

God Is Awesome

"Dominion and awe belong to God." (Job 25:2)

IN HIS MASTERPIECE *The Divine Conspiracy*, Dallas Willard writes, "Still today the Old Testament book of Psalms gives great power for faith and life. This is simply because it preserves a conceptually rich language about God and our relationships to him. If you busy yourself in Psalms, you emerge knowing God and understanding life."[1]

In the Psalter God emerges as awesome. This adjective suggests that God inspires awe. The noun awe, in reference to the Divine, means reverential or respectful fear. "Say to God, 'How awesome are your deeds! So great is your power that your enemies cringe before you. All the earth bows down to you; they sing praise to you, they sing praise to your name'" (Ps 66:3–4).

The Hebrew singular *no-raw*, "awesome," and its plural counterpart *no-raw-oat* occur fifteen times in the Psalms. To these occurrences we now turn.

AN AWESOME GOD

Psalms 47:2 and 68:35 assert that the Divine is awesome. "How awesome is the LORD Most High, the great king over all the earth!" (47:2). "You are awesome, O God, in your sanctuary; the God of Israel gives power and strength to his people" (68:35).

God inspires awe within Israel, where he dwells enthroned as king of his covenant people. But God also inspires awe throughout all the earth (see 47:1), over which he is "the great king." This notion that God's rule is boundless is unique in the theologies of the ancient world. The

---

1. Willard, *Divine Conspiracy*, 65.

rule of *other* deities was perceived as limited by the geographical realm of a god's city or nation.

Re may have inspired awe in Egypt. Bel or Marduk may have inspired fear or dread in Babylon. But their respective empires were defined by geographical borders. Not so with the LORD Most High. In fact, Psalm 76:11 invites "all the neighboring lands" to "bring gifts to the One to be feared." The word translated here "to be feared" comes from the same verbal root as the word "awesome." Psalm 99:3 invites the nations to praise the "great and awesome name" of the LORD.

Since God's rule is universal, that is to say, bound neither by space nor time, "he is to be feared above all gods" (96:4). The word here translated "feared" is *no-raw*. Ultimately, God alone is awesome: "You alone are to be feared [*no-raw*]" (76:7). "For who in the skies above can compare with the LORD? Who is like the LORD among the heavenly beings? In the council of the holy ones God is greatly feared; he is more awesome than all who surround him" (89:6–7).

AWESOME DEEDS

In Exodus 34:10 the following divine promise is made to Israel: "I am making a covenant with you. Before all your people I will do wonders never before done in any nation in all the world. The people you live among will see how awesome [*no-raw*] is the work that I, the LORD, will do for you." The Psalter, as expected, praises God for his awesome deeds done on Israel's behalf.

Psalm 66:3, 5–6 remembers the awe-inspiring miracle at the Red Sea. "Say to God, 'How awesome are your deeds! So great is your power that your enemies cringe before you.' . . . Come and see what God has done, how awesome his works in man's behalf! *He turned the sea into dry land, they passed through the waters on foot—come, let us rejoice in him*" (see 106:22—"awesome deeds by the Red Sea").

Psalm 111:6–9 remembers the awe-inspiring gifts of law and land. "He has shown his people the power of his works, giving them the lands of other nations. The works of his hands are faithful and just; all his precepts are trustworthy. They are steadfast for ever and ever, done in faithfulness and uprightness. He provided redemption for his people; he ordained his covenant forever—holy and awesome is his name."

Psalm 65:5 remembers God's awe-inspiring deeds of righteousness. "You answer us with awesome deeds of righteousness, O God our Savior, the hope of all the ends of the earth and of the farthest seas."

David commits himself and his generation to praising the "awesome works/great deeds" of God. "Great is the LORD and most worthy of praise; his greatness no one can fathom. One generation will commend your works to another; they will tell of your mighty acts. They will speak of the glorious splendor of your majesty, and I will meditate on your wonderful works. They will tell of the power of your awesome works, and I will proclaim your great deeds. They will celebrate your abundant goodness and joyfully sing of your righteousness" (145:3–7).

Israel's history was God's public arena to display his awesome work. But God's awesome work was also carried out privately in the quiet of the womb. David praises God because "I am fearfully and wonderfully [*no-raw-oat*] made" (139:14).

One Exception

Only one reference in the Psalter uses our adjective in a human context. Psalm 45:4 exhorts the right hand of the king to "display awesome deeds."

Here, then, is a book-by-book layout of the fifteen references.

Book 1	Book 2	Book 3	Book 4	Book 5
Pss 1–41	Pss 42–72	Pss 73–89	Pss 90–106	Pss 107–150
	45:4; 47:2; 65:5; 66:3, 5; 68:35	76:7, 12; 89:7	96:4; 99:3; 106:22	111:9; 139:14; 145:6

Psalm 47

Second Samuel 6 recounts how David and Israel brought up the ark of the LORD to Jerusalem to make that city God's dwelling. The past tense (in Hebrew the perfect), "God has ascended," in Psalm 47:6 must assuredly revisit that important day in David's career. In fact, the balance of v. 6, "amid shouts of joy, the LORD amid the sounding of trumpets," echoes 2 Sam 6:15.

The ark of the LORD, or the more familiar, "ark of the covenant," which was placed in the holiest sanctum ("Holy of Holies") of the tabernacle or the temple, was viewed as God's throne (1 Sam 4:4). This throne was fittingly overlain "with pure gold, both inside and out" (Exod 25:10).

Psalm 47 celebrates the enthronement of God within Israel.[2] God is king in Israel. God is "our king" (47:6). As king God acted on behalf of his subjects: He subdued Israel's enemies and gifted her with a land. "He subdued nations under us, peoples under our feet. He chose our inheritance for us, the pride of Jacob, whom he loved" (47:3-4). The subjugation of Israel's enemies makes those subject peoples vassals of God. As vassals they must praise or acknowledge the sovereignty of God's kingship.

Psalm 47 also celebrates the worldwide rule of God. "How awesome is the LORD Most High, *the great king over all the earth!*" (47:2). "For God is *the King of all the earth*" (47:7). "*God reigns over the nations*" (47:8).

Psalm 47 celebrates, then, the singular reign of God within one world. The nobles of the nations, the kings of the earth, are adopted as sons of the covenant that binds God to Israel (47:9). "The nobles of the nations assemble as the people of the God of Abraham, for the kings of the earth belong to God" (47:9; see also Gen 12:3; Gal 3:6-9).[3]

God is awesome indeed. "How awesome is the LORD Most High, the great king over all the earth!" (47:2).

Psalm 47 is a skillfully crafted song. Verses 1 and 6 (in Hebrew verses 2 and 7) invite us to praise. Verses 2-5 and 7-9 (in Hebrew 3-6 and 8-10) provide the lyric of that praise. In Hebrew each of these sections begins with the same particle (kî = key), signaling a first and second stanza in our song. Verses 2 and 7, the opening verses in each stanza/section, speak of God as King.

The singular rule of God in our world is suggested by the divine name "LORD Most High" (47:2). LORD is the covenant (or personal) name of Israel's God. "Most High" (Elyon) is used by Melchizedek in his blessing of Abram (Gen 14:19, 20). Notice that the title implies God's

---

2. Psalm 47 is usually classified as an enthronement psalm, together with Pss 93, 95-99. For a concise treatment of these psalms, consult Bullock, *Encountering the Book of Psalms*, 187-97.

3. In his book *Doors of Perception: A Guide to Reading the Psalms*, Peter R. Ackroyd writes, "The rulers, with whom their peoples are associated, are described as actually becoming God's people, associated with the tradition of God's ancient calling of Abraham to be the founder of his people. They are, as it were, adopted into the one community. Small wonder that the psalm ends with an interjection of praise, acknowledging God to be the supremely exalted one" (63).

ownership or rule of the cosmos: "Blessed be Abram by God Most High, Creator (or Possessor) of heaven and earth" (Gen 14:19, 22).

God's ownership of heaven is suggested in Psalm 57:2–3: "I cry out to God Most High, to God, who fulfills his purpose for me. He sends from heaven and saves me, rebuking those who hotly pursue me; God sends his love and faithfulness."

Psalm 83:18 testifies to God's authority over the earth: "Let them know that you, whose name is the LORD—that you alone are the Most High over all the earth." Psalm 97:9 echoes this very thought: "For you, O LORD, are the Most High over all the earth; you are exalted far above all gods."

Because God alone is awesome, we worship him with reverential or respectful fear. "Let all the earth fear the LORD; let all the people of the world revere him" (33:8; see also 119:120).

If we fear the awesome Lord, then who or what is really left to fear? David asks, "The LORD is my light and my salvation—whom shall I fear?" (27:1). "In God I trust; I will not be afraid. What can man do to me?" (56:11; see also 118:6). David need not fear the enemy drawn up against him (3:6; 27:3; 49:5), nor, for that matter, fear any evil (23:4; 91:5–6; 112:7). "We will not fear, though the earth gives way and the mountains fall into the heart of the sea" (46:2).

If we fear the awesome Lord, then we are richly blessed. "Those who fear him lack nothing" (34:9; see also 34:10), including forgiveness of sin (130:4), a trustworthy God (40:3; 56:3), and a vital role to play in God's plan for the salvation of the nations (67:7; see also 64:9; 65:8; 102:15). "Teach me your way, O LORD, and I will walk in your truth; give me an undivided heart, that I may fear your name" (86:11).

NEW TESTAMENT PARALLEL

Twelve times in the Gospels we read the words "they were filled with awe"/"they were terrified" (or some similar translation). In these contexts a crowd is filled with fear or awe for one of four reasons: (1) The crowd has just witnessed Jesus perform a miraculous healing. In Matthew 9, when Jesus healed a paralytic, the crowd was "filled with awe" (9:8). After Jesus healed a demon-possessed man, the townspeople saw the man and were afraid (Mark 5:15; Luke 8:35). (2) The disciples are learning just who Jesus is. At the transfiguration of Jesus in Matthew 17, Peter, James, and John hear the voice of God saying, "This is my Son, whom I love;

with him I am well pleased. Listen to him!" (17:5). When they heard these words, "they fell facedown to the ground, terrified" (17:6; Luke 9:34). The disciples' understanding of Jesus grows through witnessing a miracle. After Jesus calmed the storm, the disciples were terrified, and they asked each other, "Who is this? Even the wind and the waves obey him" (Mark 4:41). When the disciples saw Jesus walking on the water, they were terrified (John 6:19). (3) The chief priests and Pharisees were afraid of Jesus' popularity (Matt 21:46; Mark 12:12; Luke 20:19). The crowds esteemed Jesus to be at least a prophet. (4) Others realize who Jesus is. At the crucifixion of Jesus, many were terrified and exclaimed, "Surely he was the Son of God" (Matt 27:54). The shepherds were terrified at the appearing of the angel who came to announce the birth of the Savior (Luke 2:9).

Do we treat Jesus with contempt, as the chief priests and Pharisees did? Or do we worship him as our awesome God who has done awesome deeds?

∽

"If you busy yourself in Psalms, you emerge knowing God." How does one busy oneself in a psalm or in a characteristic of God? You study, you meditate, you sing, and you pray.

MEDITATION

- On what mighty deeds of God found in the Old Testament will you meditate?
- What do these deeds of righteousness reveal about God?
- Now enter God's presence with respectful fear. Spend some time on your knees, praising and thanking God for these wonderful deeds. For what are you thanking Him?

MUSICAL REFLECTION

In 1886 Carl Bobert, a Swedish pastor, wrote the lyrics to my favorite hymn, "How Great Thou Art."

> O Lord my God, When I in awesome wonder,
> Consider all the worlds Thy Hands have made;
> I see the stars, I hear the rolling thunder,

Thy power throughout the universe displayed.
Then sings my soul, My Savior God, to Thee,
How great Thou art, How great Thou art.
Then sings my soul, My Savior God, to Thee,
How great Thou art, How great Thou art!

In 1988 Richard Mullins wrote the song, "Our God is an Awesome God." Many of you can sing the chorus from memory!

PRAYER

O God, Lord Most High, you are King over all of the earth. You alone are to be feared, for great is your power—so great that your enemies cringe before you.

Let me meditate upon your wonderful works and great deeds, for they reveal who you are. And you are awesome!

Your deeds are glorious, your actions as stars, too numerous to count. They cause me to tremble in reverence before you. Yet you are my God! In my lowly state, I can call you Father and experience your love. I praise your holy name—you are great and worthy of praise.

O precious God, our Savior, hope of all eternity, there is such sweet comfort in knowing your awesomeness. Let me never forget your mighty deeds of the past, for you continue to display your acts of power on behalf of your children today. Rejoice, people of the earth. Let us praise his holy name. Let us praise his holy deeds.

∼

What are your song and your prayer?

4

God Is Creator

"In the beginning God created the heavens and the earth"
(Genesis 1:1)

THE PSALMS AFFIRM THAT God created the heavens and the earth (121:2; 124:8; 134:3; 146:6). The Psalms also affirm the same for the sea (89:9–10; 95:5; 104:25; 146:6). "The heavens are yours, and yours also the earth; you founded the world and all that is in it" (89:11).

By verbal command he brought the heavens and the earth into physical existence (33:6, 9; 148:3–5). "Let them praise the name of the LORD, for he commanded and they were created" (148:5). Though spoken into existence, yet the heavens and the earth are regarded as the work of his fingers/hands (8:3, 6; 19:1; 95:5). He made all living creatures (104:24–26), including mankind (8:5–6), who is the pinnacle of His creativity, with understanding (136:5), wisdom (104:24), power (65:6), reliability (119:89–91), glory (8:1; 19:1), and goodness (104:28).

The LORD alone maintains the life of his creation. "You care for the land and water it; you enrich it abundantly. The streams of God are filled with water to provide the people with grain, for so you have ordained it. You drench its furrows and level its ridges; you soften it with showers and bless its crops. You crown the year with your bounty, and your carts overflow with abundance. The grasslands of the desert overflow; the hills are clothed with gladness. The meadows are covered with flocks and the valleys are mantled with grain; they shout for joy and sing" (65:9–13). "He waters the mountains from his upper chambers; the earth is satisfied by the fruit of his work. He makes grass grow for the cattle, and plants for man to cultivate—bringing forth food from the earth; wine that gladdens the heart of man, oil to make his face shine, and bread that sustains his heart" (104:13–15; see also 104:27–30).

God has ordained that the sun (19:4–6; 104:19b, 22–23; 148:3), moon (104:19a, 20–21; 148:3), and stars (148:3) will remain true to their design and Designer. The same is true of Earth. "The world is firmly established; it cannot be moved" (93:1; see also 96:10; 104:5). The natural elements, including thunder, lightning, clouds, wind, and precipitation, all serve Him (29:3–9; 104:3–4; 135:7; 147:15–18). "Praise the LORD from the earth ... lightning and hail, snow and clouds, stormy winds that do his bidding" (148:7a–8). God alone determines the life span of His creatures (90:3–12; 104:27–30).

The noun "work" or "works" (GK 5126) occurs thirty-nine times. The term is used ten times to refer to some human work. The other twenty-nine refer to the work of God. God's work of creation is important to the Psalter. This theme is explicit at 8:3, 6; 19:1; 86:8–9; 102:25; 103:22; 104:13, 24, 31–32; 139:14; 145:9, 10, 17. Psalm 102:25 reads, "In the beginning you laid the foundations of the earth, and the heavens are the work of your hands." Psalm 104:24 reads, "How many are your works, O LORD! In wisdom you made them all; the earth is full of your creatures."

God's "work" in Israel's history is also celebrated. Psalm 111:6 references the work of God in driving out the inhabitants from the land promised to Israel. This work is simultaneously judgment upon sin and faithfulness to a promise. "The works of his hands are faithful and just" (111:7). The Canaanites were destroyed, as were all other enemies (66:3). In Psalm 106:13 the Exodus is in mind.

Many of the references to the work of God are not clearly defined. Context does not clarify what specific work is in mind (28:5; 33:4; 64:9; 92:4–5; 107:22, 24; 111:2; 118:17; 138:8; 143:5; 145:4).

"Praise him for his acts of power" (150:2). The noun "strength, might" (GK 1476), here "acts of power," appears seventeen times. (The corresponding adjective is used only twice of the LORD, both in 24:8.) Since the totality of humanity cannot quantify the power of God (see 40:5; 71:15), we are unable to fully declare his praise (106:2), though we must try (21:13; 71:16, 18; 145:4, 11, 12). In the Psalter just three of his acts of power come into focus. (1) God is creator. Psalm 89:11–12 notes this fact. Psalm 89:13 then adds: "Your arm is endued with power." Psalm 65:6 speaks of God as the one "who formed the mountains by your power, having armed yourself with strength." (2) God delivered his people from the Egyptians. "Yet he saved them for his name's sake, to make his mighty power known. He rebuked the Red Sea, and it dried up; he led them through the depths as through a desert" (106:8–9). Psalm 66:6 recounts how God turned the Red Sea into dry land, which allowed the Israelites to pass through the waters on foot. How powerful and awesome are God's works on behalf of his people (66:5). Psalm 66:7 reads, "He rules forever by his power." (3) Through power and authority God acts to deliver and to judge. "Save me, O God, by your name; vindicate me by your might" (54:1; see also 20:6; 80:2).

The noun (technically, it is a participle!) "wonderful acts/works" (GK 7098) appears twenty-nine times. This word focuses upon the acts of the LORD that exceed our ability to comprehend and understand. These acts are "wonders." The LORD alone performs these innumerable, miraculous wonders (72:18; 136:4). "Many, O LORD my God, are the wonders you have done ... were I to speak and tell of them, they would be too many to declare" (40:5). The Psalter uses this word to describe the awe-inspiring wonder of: (1) The Word. "Open my eyes that I may see wonderful things in your law" (119:18; see also 78:4–5; 119:27); (2) Human life. "I praise you because I am fearfully and wonderfully made; your works are wonderful" (139:14); and (3) Deliverance for the nation from Egypt (78:11–12, 32; 106:7, 22) and for the individual from the enemy (9:1, 3).

The corresponding noun (GK 7099) appears only seven times: three times translated "miracles" (77:11, 14; 78:12), three times translated "wonders" (88:10, 12; 89:5), and once "wonderful" (119:129).

The noun "strength, power" (GK 3946) appears eleven times, but only four of these relate to the LORD. He formed the mountains by his strength (65:6). The "voice of the LORD," that is, the thunder in a devastating storm, is powerful and majestic (29:4). When he gave Israel its promised land by driving out the former inhabitants, he demonstrated the "power of his works" (111:6). "He heals the brokenhearted and binds up their wounds. He determines the number of the stars and calls them each by name. Great is our LORD and mighty in power" (147:3–5a).

The adjective "mighty, numerous" (GK 6786) occurs three times (10:10; 35:18; 135:10). At 135:10 the LORD killed "mighty kings," a reference to the kings Israel vanquished as she moved from the wilderness into the land of promise (see 135:11-12). A related noun occurs at 68:35.

The noun "strength" (GK 2657) is used only three times. The LORD will respond in might against the sins of his people (59:11). When the LORD brings victory against the foe, the righteous sing out: "The LORD's right hand has done mighty things!" (118:15, 16).

A final word for "strength" is dealt with in Chapter Nine.

WHO?

The question "Who?" occurs forty-two times in the Psalms. These questions show that our God is beyond comparison. (Remember the question, "What do I know of holy?") The glorious design of our world leads us to marvel at and worship the Designer. Who, indeed, is like our God, the Creator? Many of these "Who?" questions move beyond creation, but they certainly have a basis in it.

"Who can show us any good?" (4:6a)	In spite of the way things appear, God is good and he allows us to experience that goodness. "Let the light of your face shine upon us." (4:6b)
"Who will come from Mount Zion to rescue Israel?" (14:7; *New Living Translation*). "Is there anyone around to save Israel?" (*The Message*). See also 53:6.	God alone will bring salvation. "Yes, God is around; God turns life around" (*The Message*).
"For who is God besides the LORD?" (18:31a)	The gods of Canaan, Egypt, and Mesopotamia are imposters. The LORD alone is God.
"And who is the Rock except our God?" (18:31b)	Only our God can arm us with a sense of strength and security.
"Who is this King of glory?" (24:8, 10)	The King who is returning from battle is the king who returns victoriously. He is the LORD strong and mighty, the LORD mighty in battle.
"The LORD is my light and my salvation—whom shall I fear? The LORD is the stronghold of my life—of whom shall I be afraid?" (27:1)	When there is trouble of any kind, we need not fear, for the LORD will keep us safe in his protective love.

"My whole being will exclaim, 'Who is like you, O LORD?'" (35:10)	This context focuses on the power of the LORD to rescue the poor and needy from those who have overpowered them.
"Who can hear us?" (59:7). "Who will see them?" (64:5). See also 19:12.	The evil (enemies and nations) may believe that their plans and actions go unnoticed. Utterly laughable (59:8). The LORD is mindful of all things, even those that are planned in secret.
"Who will bring me to the fortified city? Who will lead me to Edom?" (60:9; 108:10)	As David engages the Edomites in battle, these questions come to his lips. He confesses that only with God, the LORD, will he gain victory. The help of man or some imagined deity is worthless.
"Your righteousness reaches to the skies, O God, you who have done great things. Who, O God, is like you?" (71:19)	Whose work is as great as the LORD's?
"Whom have I in heaven but you? And earth has nothing I desire besides you." (73:25)	Who, besides the LORD, resides in heaven? Who else will take me into his glory? Can any earthly attraction fulfill our desires?
"Your ways, O God, are holy. What god is so great as our God?" (77:13)	This context celebrates the redemption of God's people from the supposed power of the Egyptian pantheon and Pharaoh. In the Exodus only the LORD performed miracles. Only the LORD displayed power. Just ask the Egyptians!
"For who in the skies above can compare with the LORD?" (89:6a) "O LORD God Almighty, who is like you?" (89:8a)	Just ask the angels if they are worthy of comparison to the LORD (89:6b–7).
"Who knows the power of your anger?" (90:11a). See also 76:7.	Since God's anger is always tempered by mercy, no one has seen or heard his anger in full expression.

"Who can proclaim the mighty acts of the LORD or fully declare his praise?" (106:2)	Allow me to quote John 21:25 here: "If every one of [the mighty acts of the LORD] were written down, I suppose that even the whole world would not have room for the books that would be written."
"Who is like the LORD our God, the One who sits enthroned on high, who stoops down to look on the heavens and the earth?" (113:5–6)	Is there another king who is so transcendent that he has to stoop to see the heavens and yet casts his eyes upon the poor and needy of the earth (113:7–9)?
"If you, O LORD, kept a record of sins, O Lord, who could stand?" (130:3)	Dare I apply John 21:25 to our sins? No one can stand before the LORD! But with the LORD there is forgiveness (130:4).
"He hurls down his hail like pebbles. Who can withstand his icy blast?" (147:17)	Read Joshua 10:11!

Many of the "Who" questions reveal something about how to live a life that is pleasing to the LORD. According to Psalm 107:43, the wise (Who is wise?) reflect upon "the great love of the LORD." The one who loves life (Who loves life?) "turns from evil and does good; seeks peace and pursues it" (34:12, 14; see also 12:4). "LORD, who may dwell in your sanctuary? Who may live on your holy hill?" (15:1). The remainder of the psalm provides the answers to these questions. "Who may ascend the hill of the LORD? Who may stand in his holy place?" (24:3). The answers to these questions are given in 24:4–6. "Who is the man that fears the LORD?" (25:12).

A few of these questions point out the fleeting nature of human life (an obvious contrast with the eternality of God). "Who praises you from the grave?" (6:5). "Man is a mere phantom as he goes to and fro: He bustles about, but only in vain; he heaps up wealth, not knowing *who* will get it" (39:6). "Who will rise up for me against the wicked? Who will take a stand for me against evildoers?" (94:16). Notice the psalmist's response to his own questions: "Unless the LORD had given me help, I would soon have dwelt in the silence of death" (94:17). "What (literally, "Who") man can live and not see death, or save himself from the power of the grave?" (89:48).

NEW TESTAMENT PARALLEL

The verb "create" (GK 3231) occurs fifteen times in the New Testament. (The corresponding noun "creation" occurs nineteen times.) God created the world (Mark 13:19; Eph 3:9; 1 Tim 4:3; Rev 4:11; 10:6), which, obviously, includes mankind (Matt 19:4; 1 Cor 11:9). He is, therefore, the Creator (Rom 1:25). Paul says the same of Jesus. "For by him [Jesus] all things were created: things in heaven and on earth, visible and invisible ... all things were created by him and for him" (Col 1:16).

Christ is also in the process of creating a people for himself, a people without ethnic definition (Eph 2:15), but known by its true righteousness, holiness (Eph 4:24), knowledge (Col 3:10), and good works (Eph 2:10).

The question "Who?" occurs forty-two times in the Psalms. These questions show that our God is beyond comparison. The "Who?" question in the New Testament shows that our Savior is beyond comparison.

When Jesus forgave the sins of the paralytic, some teachers of the law asked, "Who can forgive sins but God alone?" (Mark 2:7; Luke 5:21; see also Luke 7:49). After Jesus calmed the storm, his disciples asked, "Who is this? Even the wind and the waves obey him!" (Mark 4:41). After Jesus had healed a man born blind, he had opportunity to ask the man, "Do you believe in the Son of Man?" The man responded to Jesus with his own question, "Who is he, sir?" Jesus answered, "You have now seen him; in fact, he is the one speaking with you" (John 9:35-37; see also 12:34). When Jesus entered Jerusalem at the beginning of his Passion Week, the city was stirred and asked, "Who is this?" The crowds answered, "This is Jesus, the prophet from Nazareth in Galilee" (Matt 21:10).

As Paul laments his wretched state, he asks, "Who will rescue me from this body of death?" He then answers his own question: "Thanks be to God—through Jesus Christ our Lord!" (Rom 7:25). If God is for us—and he most certainly is—the crucifixion and resurrection of Jesus prove this, then who shall separate us from the love of Christ? (Rom 8:35).

John heard an angel asking, "Who is worthy to break the seals and open the scroll?" (Rev 5:2). This question is answered by one of the twenty-four elders: "The Lion of the tribe of Judah, the Root of David, has triumphed. He is able to open the scroll and its seven seals" (Rev 5:5).

"If you busy yourself in Psalms, you emerge knowing God." How does one busy oneself in a psalm or in a characteristic of God? You study, you meditate, you sing, and you pray.

MEDITATION

- Of all the wonders of God's good creation, which one for you is the most captivating? Why?
- How does the Creator provide for your daily needs?
- Which "work" in creation or in history still has you in a state of awe?
- When and where did you see the strength of the LORD?
- Which "Who" question causes you to delight in the greatness of our God?
- If you were asked, "Who is this Jesus?" what would your response be?

MUSICAL REFLECTION

In 1225 Francis of Assisi (1182–1226) penned the words that would become the lyrics for the hymn "All Creatures of Our God and King." The English translation was made by William Draper (1855–1933).

> All creatures of our God and King, lift up your voice and with us sing Alleluia, Alleluia! Thou burning sun with golden beam, thou silver moon with softer gleam: O praise Him, O praise Him! Alleluia, Alleluia! Alleluia!

> Thou rushing wind that art so strong, ye clouds that sail in heav'n along, O praise Him! Thou rising morn, in praise rejoice; ye lights of evening, find a voice: O praise Him, O praise Him! Alleluia, Alleluia! Alleluia!

> Dear mother earth, who day by day unfoldest blessings on our way, O praise Him! Alleluia! The flow'rs and fruits that in thee grow, let them His glory also show; O praise Him, O praise Him! Alleluia, Alleluia! Alleluia!

> Let all things their Creator bless, and worship Him in humbleness—O praise Him! Alleluia! Praise, praise the Father, praise the Son, and praise the Spirit, Three in One: O praise Him, O praise Him! Alleluia, Alleluia! Alleluia!

PRAYER

Our Father in heaven, hallowed be your name. We praise you for the wonders of this world you created. Thank you for the DNA helix and for the Rocky Mountains. Thank you for the smallest blade of grass and for the tallest tree. Thank you for the three toed sloth and for the cheetah. Thank you for the amoeba and for the blue whale. Thank you for the azure of the clear sky, the fire of fall's colors, the green carpets of grass, and for all of the other colors that comprise the rainbows of our lives. Thank you for the sound of a child's laughter, for the rhythmic sound of rain, for the genius of music, for spoken words, and for long-awaited good news. Thank you for the smell of fresh bread, of clean clothes right off the clothesline, of a bonfire at night, and of anything brand new. Thank you for the wonders of taste. Our hunger calls out for food, and you have satisfied that hunger with a myriad of sensations. Thank you for all who contribute to fill our lives with apples and apple pie, bread, corn-on-the-cob, Mountain Dew, oranges, peaches and peach pie, pecan rolls, pizza, rice, spaghetti, to name just a few mouth-watering delicacies. Thank you for touch: the most obvious sense of belonging to each other. Thank you for a lover's embrace, a child's hug, a dear friend's handshake, a concerned mother's hand to the face of a feverish child, and the gentle touches of affirmation. Thank you Father for creating our world of wonders and caring for it so wondrously! Amen.

∼

What are your song and your prayer?

5

God Is King

"The LORD will rule over you" (Judges 8:23)

THE TERM *KING* (GK 4889) is used sixty-seven times in Psalms. These occurrences cluster into four basic categories: (1) to describe foreign human kings (2:2, 10; 45:9; 48:4; 68:12, 14, 29; 72:10 (xx), 11; 76:12; 102:15; 105:14, 20, 30; 110:5; 119:46; 135:10, 11 (xx); 136:17, 18, 19, 20; 138:4; 148:11; 149:8); (2) to refer to the human kings of Israel and Judah (2:6; 18:51; 20:9; 21:1, 7; 45:1, 5, 11, 13, 14, 15; 61:7; 63:11; 72:1 (xx); 89:18, 27; 144:10); (3) to refer generally to kings (33:16); and (4) to describe the kingship of the LORD (5:2; 10:16; 24:7, 8, 9, 10 (xx); 29:10; 44:4; 47:2, 6, 7; 48:2; 68:24; 74:12; 84:3; 95:3; 98:6; 99:4; 145:1; 149:2).

	Book 1 Pss 1–41	Book 2 Pss 42–72	Book 3 Pss 73–89	Book 4 Pss 90–106	Book 5 Pss 107–50
Foreign kings (28)	2:2, 10	45:9, 13; 48:4; 68:12, 14, 29; 72:10 (xx), 11	76:12	102:15; 105:14, 20, 30	110:5; 119:46; 135:10, 11 (xx); 136:17, 18, 19, 20; 138:4; 148:11; 149:8
Kings of Israel or Judah (17)	2:6; 18:51; 20:9; 21:1, 7	45:1, 5, 11, 14, 15; 61:7; 63:11; 72:1 (xx)	89:18, 27		144:10

	Book 1 Pss 1–41	Book 2 Pss 42–72	Book 3 Pss 73–89	Book 4 Pss 90–106	Book 5 Pss 107–50
Kings (1)	33:16				
The kingship of the LORD (21)	5:2; 10:16; 24:7, 8, 9, 10 (xx); 29:10	44:4; 47: 2, 6, 7; 48:2; 68:24	74:12; 84:3	95:3; 98:6; 99:4	145:1; 149:2

Ps 45:13 "princess" = daughter of the king; 72:1 "royal son" = son of the king; 135:11 "kings" (NIV) = kingdoms

FOREIGN KINGS

Foreign kings who have defied the LORD (2:2) are warned (2:10) to worship (68:29; 72:10), fear (76:12), revere (102:15), heed (119:46), and praise (138:4; 148:11) the LORD. He has rebuked (105:14; see Gen 20:7) and destroyed (48:4–7) kings. He may even "crush kings on the day of his wrath" (110:5; see 149:8), as he has done in the past. Just ask Sihon, Og (135:10–11; 136:17–20), and the kings of Canaan (68:12, 14). Foreign kings should join the kings of Israel/Judah and "bow down" to the LORD (72:11).

HUMAN KINGS OF ISRAEL AND JUDAH

When the LORD promised a dynastic succession to David (2 Sam 7:11b–12), he called forth from the future each successor to the throne. This calling, this divine appointment, is heard at Psalm 2:6: "I [the LORD] have installed my King on Zion, my holy hill."

In a dynastic succession, a father passes his throne to a son, who in turn will pass it to his son, and so on. This father-son dynamic is an apt metaphor for understanding the intimacy of this divine calling. At Psalm 89:26, the king calls out to the LORD, "You are my Father." At v. 27, the LORD refers to the king as "my firstborn, the most exalted of the kings of the earth." The LORD then speaks of maintaining his love for the king forever (v. 28): "I will establish his line forever, his throne as long as the heavens endure" (v. 29).

The Old Testament proclaims that the LORD is King. The book of Psalms makes the same proclamation, but more of that a bit later. This affirmation suggests that each king of Israel/Judah is actually a co-regent, one who reigns with and on behalf of the LORD. If the LORD's style of reign is a reflection of his character, and it truly is, then each king must exhibit the same godly characteristics. Before David passed from this life, he passed his reign to Solomon with this advice, "So be strong, show yourself a man, and observe what the LORD your God requires: Walk in his ways, and keep his decrees and commands, his laws and requirements, as written in the Law of Moses, so that you may prosper in all you do and wherever you go" (1 Kings 2:2b–3; see also Deut 17:18–20).

This convergence of the king with the King's character is voiced at 72:1. "Endow the king with your justice, O God, the royal son (literally, the "son of the king") with your righteousness." Psalm 89:18 adds, "Our king [belongs] to the Holy One of Israel."

One of the duties of an ancient king was to engage the enemy in battle. Psalm 20:9 shares a simple prayer for the king in battle: "O LORD, save the king!" (see 45:5). A simple prayer indeed, but based on the trust heard in verse 6: "Now I know that the LORD saves his anointed; he answers him from his holy heaven with the saving power of his right hand."

If Psalm 20 voices a prayer for the king in battle, then Psalm 21 rejoices in answered prayer—the battle has been won. Listen to 21:1. "O LORD, the king rejoices in your strength. How great is his joy in the victories you give!" Hear the same at verse 5. "Through the victories you gave, his glory is great; you have bestowed on him splendor and majesty" (see also 21:7; 18:50; 144:10).

The great warrior David prayed for long life (61:6). His prayer was answered. In fact David's continuing praise (63:11) is proof of the answer, as is the deafening silence of his foes (63:9–10).

Psalm 45 is a wedding song. The king's lyricist (45:1) rejoices in the wedding of the most excellent of men (v. 2) to a princess (literally, "daughter of a king") who is "all glorious" (v. 13) and whose beauty enthralls the king (v. 11). Accompanied by her bridesmaids, she is led to the king (v. 14), who is in the palace (v. 15).

KINGS OR KINGSHIP

Psalm 33:16 is the only verse in this category. Perhaps I could have placed it in either of the previous categories. Whether one speaks of foreign kings or of the kings of Israel/Judah, the truth of this verse is evident.

When the LORD chooses sides in a battle, "No king is saved by the size of his army; no warrior escapes by his great strength." With a band of 300 Israelites, the LORD subdued 135,000 Midianites (Judg 8:10–11). A king's prayer led to the death of 185,000 Assyrian soldiers (Isaiah 37:36), while a prophet's prayer led to the capture of an entire force of Aramean troops (2 Kgs 6:8–23).

THE KINGSHIP OF THE LORD

The LORD is King. His reign is limitless. With respect to time, his reign is eternal. The LORD is king "for ever and ever" (10:16). The LORD is "enthroned as King forever" (29:10). With respect to space, his reign has no boundaries. He is the great King "over all the earth" (47:2, 7, 8). "In his hand are the depths of the earth, and the mountain peaks belong to him. The sea is his, for he made it, and his hands formed the dry land" (95:4–5). With respect to rivals, there are none. He is "the great King above all gods" (95:3).

As King he is expected to defend and deliver his people from their enemies. Since the King is "strong and mighty" (24:8) and "mighty in battle" (24:8), he vanquishes the foe. The King enables his troops by going with them into battle. "Through you we push back our enemies; through your name we trample our foes. I do not trust in my bow, my sword does not bring me victory; but you give us victory over our enemies, you put our adversaries to shame" (44:5–7).

He is not a king who is aloof or far removed from his subjects. David refers to him as "*my* King" (5:2; see also 84:3). Though he governs the entire world, he can be found in the city of Jerusalem (48:2), even in the sanctuary (68:24). His presence is celebrated: "shout for joy before the LORD, the King" (98:6). "Let the people of Zion be glad in their King" (149:2; see also 145:1).

Because the King is both powerful—"his greatness no one can fathom" (145:3b)—and present, he hears and responds to prayer (5:2). His responses will always be "just and right" (99:4) and redemptive (74:12).

What do we learn from the book-by-book layout of these references? We learn two things. First, God's people will always live in the context of hostile world powers (46:6–7). Foreign kings are mentioned in each of the five books of the Psalter. Second, even though the kings of Israel/Judah are hardly mentioned after Book 2, God's unmatched reign as King continues throughout all space and time.

God Is King

Psalm 146

Psalm 146 begins and ends with the summons to praise the LORD—the famous *Hallelujah*. This psalm provides some reasons why the LORD, the King, receives our praise.

Human leadership (foreign or national) can hardly compare to the reign of the LORD. His reign is eternal. "The LORD reigns forever, your God, O Zion, for all generations" (v. 10). Earthly kings are mere mortals (v. 3). At death "they return to the ground" (v. 4), powerless to save (v. 3) or to insure the reality of their best laid plans (v. 4).

The LORD, however, possesses both power and fidelity to save (v. 5) and to see his plans through to reality. As for power, he is "the Maker of heaven and earth, the sea, and everything in them" (v. 6). As for fidelity, "he remains faithful forever" (v. 6).

Verses 7–9 provide nine examples of how the LORD, true to his character as King, brings help and hope (v. 5): help for the needy and hope for the righteous (I am not implying that the needy are not righteous or the righteous never have needs).

Help for the needy	Hope for the righteous
He upholds the cause of the oppressed	
[He] gives food to the hungry	
The **LORD** sets prisoners free	
The **LORD** gives sight to the blind	
The **LORD** lifts up those who are bowed down	
	The **LORD** loves the righteous
The **LORD** watches over the alien	
[He] sustains the fatherless and the widow	
	He frustrates the ways of the wicked

The kings of the ancient world were expected to provide help for the needy and justice for the oppressed. When Absalom was undermining the authority of his father, King David, his campaign slogan was: "If only I were appointed judge in the land! Then everyone who has a complaint or case could come to me and I would see that he gets justice" (2 Sam 15:4).

Israel's true King, the LORD, was faithful to the perceived role of king. Note above the five-fold emphasis on the LORD's name.

The term Messiah (GK 5431) is often associated with a discussion of kingship. The term appears ten times in the Psalter (2:2; 18:50; 20:6; 28:8; 84:9; 89:38, 51; 105:15; 132:10, 17). The Messiah, or the Anointed One, refers either to David or to a Davidic descendent (18:50).

At 2:2 the Messiah faces opposition from certain kings/rulers (89:51). This opposition is futile, since God gives his king great victories (18:50). The LORD, "a fortress of salvation for his anointed one" (28:8), saves his anointed on the day of battle (20:6). This victory is assumed in the prayers of God's righteous people (84:9).

The moral failings of the House of David led to its historic collapse in 587/6 BC. From that point on, the nation lived under the rule of Babylon, Persia, Greece, and Rome. In those heavy days of loss and despair, the psalmist could say of God, "you have been very angry with your anointed one" (89:38).

The book of Psalms concludes though with hope for a renewed Davidic kingdom. By revisiting the past (105:15) and reviving the Davidic promise (132:10-12), the Psalter hopes and waits: "Here [Zion] I will make a horn grow for David and set up a lamp for my anointed one. I will clothe his enemies with shame, but the crown on his head will be resplendent" (132:17).

A king sits on a throne (GK 4058). The word throne appears eighteen times in the Psalter. The word is used in quotation of God's promise to establish the throne of David in perpetuity. "The LORD swore an oath to David, a sure oath that he will not revoke: 'One of your own descendants I will place on your throne—if your sons keep my covenant and the statutes I teach them, then their sons will sit on your throne for ever and ever'" (132:11-12; see also 89:3-4, 29, 36, 44).

God sits on his heavenly (11:4; 103:19), eternal (45:6; 93:2), and holy (47:8) throne, judging righteously (9:4, 7). In fact "righteousness and justice are the foundation" of His throne (89:14; 97:2).

This foundation—righteousness and justice—is to be the enduring legacy of the Davidic dynasty. Notice that God "has established his throne for judgment" (9:7). David's house was to be guarantor under God of that same justice in Israel (101:7-8; Jer 21:12). The thrones of the house of David stand "for judgment" (122:5). A corrupt throne, one that brings misery by its decrees (94:20), has no alliance with God.

A king may measure justice by his treatment of the fatherless and the widow. God, "a father to the fatherless" (68:5), helps (10:14), defends (10:18), and sustains (146:9) the fatherless. He demands that his co-regent, the king, "defend the cause of the weak and fatherless" (82:3; notice the opposite at 94:6). God, "a defender of widows" (68:5), sustains them (146:9).

A king has a crown and a scepter. God is not portrayed in the Psalms with either a crown or a scepter. He has relinquished these tokens of authority to his co-regents. The verb "to crown" (GK 6497) does occur three times. The LORD has crowned mankind with the honor of dominion and authority over the created realm (8:5). Each year the LORD crowns the fields with a bountiful harvest (65:11). The LORD crowns the faithful with love and compassion (103:4).

Two different nouns for crown appear in the Psalter. The first noun (GK 6498) appears only at 21:3. The second noun (GK 5694) appears in 89:39 and 132:18. The crown "signifies the manifestation and completion of the king's election."[1] The king bears the scepter as well (45:6; 110:2; 125:3). (The NIV offers the following at 149:4b: "he crowns the humble with salvation." The NIV's "crowns" is actually the verb "to beautify, glorify." This verb appears only this one time in the Psalms. This verb [GK 6995] is related to a noun "headdress, turban" [GK 6996], and thus the rationale for the NIV translation.)

A king has an army. The Hebrew noun "army" (GK 7372) is drawn from the verbal root "wage war, serve as soldier." An army consists of the personnel (soldiers) necessary to carry out the campaigns (wars) of the king. Israel considered the LORD to be king and therefore understood that he waged war against the enemies of his people.

One of the names for God in the Psalms is translated "LORD Almighty" (NIV) or "LORD of Hosts" (KJV). The "Almighty" in this name is a translation of the Hebrew plural of the word "army." So, literally, God is "LORD of armies." As King of Israel, he was commander-in-chief of the army/armies of Israel. The NET Bible translates, "The Lord who commands armies." Three times in the Psalms the armies of Israel are specifically mentioned (44:9; 60:10; 108:11), and each time

---

1. Keel, *The Symbolism of the Biblical World: Ancient Near Eastern Iconography and the Book of Psalms*, 259.

Israel's commander-in-chief is missing: "you no longer go out with our armies." (The noun "armies" also appears at 68:12, but this is a reference to Canaanite armies.)

The "of Hosts" in the King James Version needs explanation. A "host" is "a multitude or great number of persons or things" (dictionary.com). What could this great number of persons or things be? First, as we saw above, it could refer to a number of soldiers, an army. Second, it could refer to a number of angels, that is an angelic or a heavenly host. Note the parallelism in 148:2. "Praise him, all his angels, praise him, all his heavenly hosts." The same parallelism exists in 103:20-21. "Praise the LORD, you his angels, you mighty ones who do his bidding, who obey his word. Praise the LORD, all his heavenly hosts, you his servants who do his will." In *The Message* Eugene Peterson offers "God-of-the-Angel-Armies." The *New Living Translation* offers "The Lord of Heaven's Armies." Third, it could refer to a number of stars, a starry host. "By the word of the LORD were the heavens made, their starry host by the breath of his mouth."

"LORD Almighty" occurs fifteen times in the Psalter (24:10; 46:7, 11; 48:8; 59:5; 69:6; 80:4, 7, 14, 19; 84:1, 3, 8, 12; 89:8). The context of these eight psalms suggests that the LORD Almighty is Israel's victorious Warrior-King. The LORD Almighty is "the King of glory" (24:10), who is "mighty in battle" (24:8). The LORD Almighty "makes wars cease to the ends of the earth; he breaks the bow and shatters the spear, he burns the shields with fire" (46:9). "When the kings joined forces, when they advanced together . . . you destroyed them like ships of Tarshish shattered by an east wind" (48:4, 7). "Rouse yourself to punish all the nations; show no mercy to wicked traitors" (59:5). "Pour out your wrath on them; let your fierce anger overtake them" (69:24).

Ten times in the Psalter we hear the request "Arise, O LORD/God" (3:7; 7:6; 9:19; 10:12; 17:13; 35:2; 44:26; 74:22; 82:8; 132:8; GK 7756). The psalmists charge (it is an imperative, the command form) the Warrior-King to act in judgment and deliverance. "Arise, O LORD, let not man triumph; let the nations be judged in your presence. Strike them with terror, O LORD; let the nations know they are but men" (9:19-20).

A similar request comes from the verb "rouse oneself, awake" (GK 6424). This verb occurs twelve times in the Psalms. Five of these refer to human activity (57:8 [three times] and 108:3 [twice]). The other seven refer then to the work of God as Warrior-King on behalf of his people. "Awake, my God; decree justice" (7:6). Since God does not tire and requires rest, this is synonymous with the petition "save me" or "help me." "Awake, and rise to my defense!" (35:23; see also 44:23; 59:4; 73:20; 78:38). "Awaken your might; come and save us" (80:2).

"Sleep" may be metaphoric for the apparent hiddenness of God and consequent abandonment of Israel (44:23; 78:65). But the LORD is active; he has not abandoned his people. "Indeed, he who watches over Israel will neither slumber nor sleep" (121:4).

A king has a kingdom and with it "sovereignty" and "dominion." These abstract nouns are not common in the Psalter: three different nouns occurring twelve times. The LORD's kingdom "rules over all" (103:19). His kingdom is glorious (145:11, 12), everlasting (145:13), and cosmic (136:8–9). "Dominion belongs to the LORD and he rules over the nations" (22:28; see also 103:22), which, of course, includes Israel and Judah (114:2).

A king has a capital city. The Warrior-King has established a city as his city. This is, of course, the city of Jerusalem. Because it is his city, we are right in calling it "The City of God/the LORD." This title is used six times in the Psalter (46:4; 48:1, 8 [twice]; 87:3; 101:8), and only one other time in the rest of the Old Testament (Isa 60:14). Jerusalem is the "holy place where the Most High dwells" (46:4). It is his "holy mountain" (48:1). Jerusalem is oft times called Zion.

The noun Zion (GK 7482) appears thirty-eight times in the Psalter. The LORD dwells in Zion (74:2; 76:2; 132:13; 135:21) and is enthroned there (9:11; 48:2; 99:2; 146:10). It is a fortified city (48:12; 51:18), characterized by security (125:1; 129:5), blessing (128:5; 133:3; 134:3), joy (48:11; 97:8; 137:1, 3; 149:2), and worship (9:14; 65:1; 84:7; 102:21; 147:12). The LORD loves Zion (78:68; 87:2). Salvation/help comes out from Zion (14:7; 20:2; 53:6), from whence God shines (50:2). The LORD will restore/save Zion (69:35; 87:5; 102:13, 16). In fact, he already has (126:1)! It is a city from whence the messiah rules (2:6; 110:2). It is, of course, the city of Jerusalem, home to the temple of the LORD!

A king "reigns" (GK 4887). This verb is found only six times in the Psalms and always in reference to God (47:8) or to the LORD (93:1; 96:10; 97:1; 99:1; 146:10). Since he is King of all the earth (47:2, 7), he reigns over the nations (47:8), including Israel. Since he is not bound by time, his reign predates creation past (93:2) and will extend into eternity future (146:10). James L. Mays opines that the declaration "The LORD reigns" involves "a vision of reality that is the theological center of the Psalter ... The psalmic understanding of the people of God, the city of God, the king [sic] of God, and the law of God depends on its validity and implications. The psalmic functions of praise, prayer, and instruction are responses to it and articulations of its wonder, hope, and guidance."[2]

A second verb "rule, reign" (GK 5440) occurs ten times, but only half of these refer to the LORD's rule (22:28; 59:13; 66:7; 89:9; 103:19). The LORD rules over the natural realm (89:9), his people (59:13), and the nations (22:28). He rules forever by his power (66:7). "The LORD has established his throne in heaven, and his kingdom rules over all" (103:19). The other five references are: 8:6; 19:13; 105:20, 21; 106:41.

The noun "kinship, royalty," translated "dominion" by NIV at 22:28, occurs only once in the Psalms.

A king has a court of attendees. The LORD has a heavenly court: the angels do his bidding (103:20). The noun "angel" (GK 4855) appears eight times. Angels praise the LORD (103:20; 148:2). They protect or guard God's people (34:7; 91:9–12); they drive away and pursue the foes of His people (35:5, 6; 78:49).

A king has servants. The term "servant" or "servants" (GK 6269) occurs fifty-seven times in the Psalms. The term "servant" is used of individuals, such as Abraham (105:6, 42), Moses (105:26), and David (78:70; 89:3; 132:10; 144:10). The term is used collectively of the nation of Israel (136:22). The expression "servant of the LORD" is used only of David, both times in superscriptions (18; 36). The plural "servants" is very common, often referring to the righteous (34:22; 102:28; 135:14). The expression "servants of the LORD" appears only twice (113:1; 134:1).

Any king, David or otherwise, who is seeking to be a true servant of the LORD, will echo the words of 119:124–125. "Deal with your servant according to your love and teach me your decrees. I am your servant, give me discernment that I may understand your statutes."

Servants bow before their king. The verb "bow down" (GK 2556) occurs seventeen times in the Psalms. David bows before the LORD (5:7; 138:2), as do fellow Israelites (95:6; 99:5, 9; 132:7). Since foreign and false gods bow before the LORD (97:7), Israel would be senseless to worship them, though she often did (106:19), breaking God's express command (81:9). "All the earth" bows down to the LORD (66:4; 96:9), as do its nations (86:9), and their families (22:27).

---

2. Mays, *The Lord Reigns: A Theological Handbook to the Psalms*, 22.

God Is King

A second verb "bow down" (GK 4156) occurs just seven times, but only two speak of prostration before the LORD (22:29; 95:6).

If a worshipper stays for a prolonged period of time in the LORD's presence, prostration would give way to a more relaxed pose, such as sitting (2 Sam 7:18) or kneeling (Ps 95:6). At Psalm 3:3 David refers to God as the one who "lifts up my head." If David has relaxed his pose in worship, from prostration to sitting, then his gaze has risen from the dust of the floor to the gracious face of God.

NEW TESTAMENT PARALLEL

The term "king" (GK 995) is used 115 times in the NT. Saul (Acts 13:21), David (Matt 1:6), and unnamed Israelite kings (Luke 10:24) bear the title. Melchizedek (Heb 7:1), Pharaoh (Acts 7:10), Herod (Matt 2:1), Caesar (John 19:15), Agrippa (Acts 25:13), Aretas (2 Cor 11:32), and various unnamed Gentile kings (Luke 22:25) also bear the title.

God, the Great King (Matt 5:35), is hailed as "the King eternal, immortal, invisible, the only God" (1 Tim 1:17), "the blessed and only Ruler, the King of kings and Lord of lords" (1 Tim 6:15).

Jesus is also King, the King of the ages (Rev 15:3). He was born king of the Jews (Matt 2:2). He was hailed as the coming King of Zechariah's prophecy (Matt 21:5; see Zech 9:9). At his trial he was asked, "Are you the king of the Jews?" (Matt 27:11). He was charged as KING OF THE JEWS (Matt 27:37). He was declared to be the King of Israel (John 1:49; 12:13). As the King, the Lord of lords and King of kings (Rev 17:14; see 19:16), he is ruler of the kings of the earth (Rev 1:5), with power to judge and to reward (Matt 25:34, 40; see Rev 19:17–21).

The disciples were told that they would bear witness to Jesus before governors and kings (Matt 10:18; Mark 13:9; Luke 21:12), who will defy the authority of Jesus (Acts 4:25–26 quoting Psalm 2:1–2), only to cower in fear before him (Rev 6:15–17). Paul was commissioned to carry the name of Jesus "before the Gentiles and their kings" (Acts 9:15).

Christians are to pray for kings "that we may live peaceful and quiet lives" (1 Tim 2:2). Christians are to submit to the authority of kings (1 Pet 2:13) and to honor the king (1 Pet 2:17).

"If you busy yourself in Psalms, you emerge knowing God." How does one busy oneself in the psalms or in a characteristic of God? You study, you meditate, you sing, and you pray.

MEDITATION

- Where do you see hostile world powers at work today? What is the nature of God's present reign?
- Where do you see God bringing help to the needy? How?
- What do you wish God would arise and do?
- How do you serve the King? In your service, are you trying to become great, or are you serving a great King?
- Do we impoverish our worship services by avoiding bowing? Would our worship be enriched by bowing?
- If you were asked by God to write the final act of this world's story, how would you depict the kings of the world (past and present) when they see the true King, Jesus Christ?

The noun "heavens" (GK 9028) occurs seventy-four times in the Psalter. God is in heaven (115:3; 136:26; 139:8). His Word stands firm in the heavens (119:89). *He is enthroned in heaven* (2:4; 11:4; 103:19; 123:1). He looks down from the heavens (14:2; 33:13; 53:2; 80:14; 85:11; 102:19; 113:6), and He answers from heaven (20:6). He thunders (18:13) and pronounces judgment (76:8) from heaven. His love reaches to (36:5; 57:10) or surpasses (108:4) the heavens. The LORD made the heavens (8:3; 33:6; 96:5; 102:25; 104:2; 115:15; 121:2; 124:8; 134:3; 136:5; 146:6). His glory is above the heavens (8:1; 113:4; 148:13), and so he is exalted above them (57:5; 108:5).

God does reign from heaven, but his reign is also evident here. The Old Testament temple was an evidence of his earthly reign. "The temple is a part of earth which reaches into the heavens—or a part of heaven that touches the earth."[3]

Is it easier for you to think of God reigning from heaven than from earth? Why? What evidence is there for God's present rule here? What evidence might suggest otherwise?

---

3. Keel, 171.

God Is King

MUSICAL REFLECTION

In his song "Amazing Love," Chris Tomlin marvels that Christ, the King, would be condemned to die so that we can live. That is Amazing Love!

Two Anglican clergymen—Matthew Bridges (1800–1894) and Godfrey Thring (1823–1903)—contributed to the hymn "Crown Him with Many Crowns."

> Crown Him with many crowns, the Lamb upon His throne: Hark! how the heav'nly anthem drowns all music but its own! Awake, my soul, and sing of Him who died for thee, and hail Him as thy matchless King thru all eternity.

> Crown Him the Lord of love: Behold His hands and side—rich wounds, yet visible above, in beauty glorified; no angel in the sky can fully bear that sight, but downward bends his wond'ring eye at mysteries so bright.

> Crown Him the Lord of life: Who triumphed o'er the grave, who rose victorious to the strife for those He came to save; His glories now we sing, who died and rose on high, who died eternal life to bring and lives that death may die.

> Crown Him the Lord of heav'n: One with the Father known; One with the Spirit thru Him giv'n from yonder glorious throne. To Thee be endless praise, for Thou for us hast died; be Thou, O Lord, thru endless days adored and magnified.

PRAYER

Our Father in heaven, our King, we know that kings and presidents and human governments are all passing fancies. But you are the Eternal One. They may disappoint and fail us, but you are forever faithful to your people. We praise you for being help for the needy and hope for the righteous. Arise, O Lord, and free your people from oppressive regimes, from hopeless despair, and from the dictates of the Evil One. Arise, O King, the Lord Almighty, and destroy the malevolent forces which seek to plunge our world into the blackest evil. May the whole earth be filled with your glory! Come, Lord Jesus.

We bow before your throne, grateful that you have been mighty to save. We are honored to serve you, our King. May our service bring praise to your royal name. May you be praised both now and forevermore.

Come, King Jesus and usher in eternity in its glorious splendor. We long for that new city, where our walls are called Salvation and our gates Praise. Amen and Amen.

∼

What are your song and your prayer?

6

God Is Refuge

"Blessed are all who take refuge in him" (Psalm 2:12)

A NUMBER OF IMPORTANT terms are used in the Psalter to depict the protection or safety that the Lord alone offers. Among those terms under review in this chapter are "refuge," "shield," "rock," and "fortress."

REFUGE

The verb "seek refuge" (GK 2879) occurs twenty-five (25) times in twenty psalms. *The sphere of refuge is always the LORD*. Psalm 18:2a illustrates the point: "The LORD is my rock, my fortress and my deliverer; my God is my rock, in whom I take refuge." Here is the catalog of verses: 2:12; 5:11; 7:1; 11:1; 16:1; 17:7; 18:2, 30; 25:20; 31:1, 19; 34:8, 22; 36:7; 37:40; 57:1 (twice); 61:4; 64:10; 71:1; 91:4; 118:8, 9; 141:8; 144:2.[1]

With the exception of the three anonymous psalms (71, 91, and 118), David writes these "refuge psalms."[2] Since David's enemies loom large in the Psalter, one is not surprised to find David finding refuge in the LORD.

"O LORD my God, I take refuge in you; save and deliver me from all who pursue me, or they will tear me like a lion and rip me to pieces with no one to rescue me" (7:1–2; see also 17:12; [22:13] 57:4). "See how my enemies have increased and how fiercely they hate me! Guard my

---

1. The noun "refuge" (GK 4726) occurs twelve times (14:6; 46:1; 61:3; 62:7, 8; 71:7; 73:28; 91:2, 9; 94:22; 104:18; 142:5). Psalm 46:1 expresses ultimate confidence in the ultimate refuge: "God is our refuge and strength, an ever present help in trouble." Psalm 104:18—"The high mountains belong to the wild goats; the crags are a refuge for the coneys"—is the only exception to the rule that God alone is a refuge.

2. In the Septuagint (LXX) Psalms 71 and 91 are attributed to David.

life and rescue me; let me not be put to shame, for I take refuge in you" (25:19–20).

The enemies of the psalmists are compared to lions, bulls, serpents, and dogs. Four different words for "lion" appear in the Psalms (only thirteen total occurrences). The lion lies in wait (10:9; 17:12), hungry for prey (17:12; see also 104:21). Then suddenly the lion pounces, tearing its prey (7:2; 22:13; see also 57:4). Accordingly, the psalmist begs for deliverance. "Rescue me from the mouth of the lions" (22:21; see also 35:17). "Tear out, O LORD, the fangs of the lions" (58:6).

Psalm 22:12 compares the psalmist's foes to the powerful bull. "Many bulls surround me; strong bulls of Bashan encircle me" (two different words for bull are found in this verse; this is the only verse where these words are used of David's foes). Verse 13 follows: "Roaring lions tearing their prey open their mouths wide against me."

The term "serpent" appears twice in the Psalms. David speaks of the venom of his adversary (58:4). He also says that their tongues are as sharp as a serpent's (140:3). The term "dog" appears five times in the Psalms: hunting dogs in Psalm 22:16, 20 (see also 68:23) and street dogs in 59:6, 14.

The wicked and godless adversary may be likened to a lion, bull, serpent, or dog. These pariahs crave the life of the psalmist, not his possessions or his position (such as king). "The wicked plot against the righteous and gnash their teeth at them.... The wicked draw the sword and bend the bow to bring down the poor and needy, to slay those whose ways are upright" (37:12, 14).

In addition to terms like lion, bull, serpent, and dog, the foes of the individual psalmists and of the nation are called "enemies" (GK 367), "haters" (GK 8533), "foes" (GK 7675), "adversaries" (GK 7756), "pursuers" (GK 8103), "evildoers" (GK 8317), and the "wicked" (GK 8401).

Psalm 17

In verse 1 David cries out, "Give ear to my prayer." Verse 6 repeats this cry: "I call on you, O God, for you will answer me; give ear to me and hear my prayer." David's prayer is a two-fold petition: first for protection from his enemies and then for an overthrow of those enemies.

David's plea for protection comes first. "Show the wonder of your great love, you who save by your right hand those who take refuge in you from their foes. Keep me as the apple of your eye; hide me in the shadow of your wings from the wicked who assail me, from my mortal enemies who surround me" (vv. 7-9).

This plea is followed by his desire to see the overthrow of his enemies. "Rise up, O LORD, confront them, bring them down; rescue me from the wicked by your sword. O LORD, by your hand save me from such men, from men of this world whose reward is in this life" (vv. 13-14).

The first half of David's petition is separated from the second half by a vivid account of his enemies. "They close up their callous hearts, and their mouths speak with arrogance. They have tracked me down, they now surround me, with eyes alert, to throw me to the ground. They are like a lion hungry for prey, like a great lion crouching in cover" (vv. 10-12).

The translation "apple of [your] eye" is literally "the little man of the eye," because an image in miniature of one's self is seen when looking into another's eyes (see Deut 32:10). David's image in miniature is mirrored in the eye of God! To give greater emphasis to this figure, David adds "the [little] daughter of the eye" (not seen, of course, in the NIV translation).[3]

Then follows another figure, taken from the eagle (Deut 32:11), which hides its young under its wings. Delitzsch writes, "God's wings are the spreading out, i.e. the manifestations of His love, taking the creature under the protection of its intimate fellowship, and the 'shadow' of these wings is the refreshing rest and security which the fellowship of this love affords to those, who hide themselves beneath it, from the heat of outward or inward conflict."[4]

---

3. At 63:8 David proclaims, "My soul clings to you" (see 119:31). The verb translated "cling" (GK 1815) here occurs seven other times in the Psalter. Twice the verb is used to refer to the tongue sticking to the roof of the mouth (22:15; 137:6). At Psalm 102:5, where the NIV has, "I am reduced to skin and bones," the Hebrew literally reads, "My bones stick/cling to my skin." Twice the psalmist's deathlike experiences are likened to the dust of death clinging to his mortal body (44:25; 119:25). So, when David says his soul clings to God, he has drawn so close to the Divine that he has become tangible. With respect to this palpable presence, David adds, "I sing in the shadow of your wings. ... Your right hand upholds me" (63:7b, 8b).

4. Delitzsch, *Psalms*, 239.

Psalm 57

When David had fled from Saul into the cave, he was seeking refuge. David is quick to point out that his refuge was not the cave itself, but his God. "Have mercy on me, O God, have mercy on me, for in you my soul takes refuge. I will take refuge in the shadow of your wings until the disaster has passed" (v. 1).

In verse 4, David likens his enemies to lions: "I am in the midst of lions; I lie among ravenous beasts—men whose teeth are spears and arrows, whose tongues are sharp swords."

In verse 5, and then repeated at verse 11, David looks up from his personal distress to pray that God "be exalted above the heavens." It is this freeing perspective that dominates the second half of the psalm: "My heart is steadfast, O God, my heart is steadfast; I will sing and make music. Awake, my soul! Awake, harp and lyre! I will awaken the dawn. I will praise you, O Lord, among the nations; I will sing of you among the peoples. For great is your love, reaching to the heavens; your faithfulness reaches to the skies" (vv. 7–10).

The references to "heavens" in verses 3, 5, 10, and 11 suggest divine resources that save David from personal crisis: "He sends from heaven and saves me" (v. 3). "For great is your love, reaching to the heavens; your faithfulness reaches to the skies" (v. 10).

Psalm 61

This psalm is first a prayer for security (vv. 1–4) and then a thanksgiving for the assured answer (vv. 5–8).

Forced to flee from Absalom's coup, David felt he had been banished to the "ends of the earth" (v. 2). The consequent feelings of homelessness and separation from the abode of God overwhelmed David—"I call as my heart grows faint."[5] "A rock of difficulties still ever lies before him which is too high for his natural strength, for his human ability, therefore insurmountable. But he is of good courage: God will lead him up with a sure step, so that, removed from all danger, he will have rocky ground under his feet."[6]

---

5. The verb translated here as "faint" can be used in contexts where there is great stress and death seems near (Pss 77:3; 102:1; 107:5; 142:3; 143:4; Jonah 2:7).

6. Delitzsch, 202–3.

David is confident of God's protection, though, for God has already proved Himself to be a refuge (v. 3). Kidner has noted how God's safe keeping is viewed in increasingly personal terms, as the high crag of verse 2 gives place to the tower of verse 3, and this in turn to the hospitality of the tent (v. 4), and finally the affectionate shelter symbolized by "your wings."[7]

God's assurance dawns upon David in verse 5—"For you have heard my vows, O God; you have given me the heritage of those who fear your name." Vows were usually made good in a single ceremony (Jonah 2:9), but David realizes that he can never repay God for this sense of security: "Then will I ever sing praise to your name and fulfill my vows day after day" (v. 8).

SHIELD

The term "shield" (GK 4482) occurs nineteen times in the Psalter. Six of these refer either to earthly kings (47:9; 84:9; 89:18) or to an actual weapon of war (18:35; 35:2; 76:3).

The remaining thirteen occurrences are used of God as the shield of the faithful. Wilson describes the metaphor as follows: "The term *magen* used here normally refers to a smaller round shield held in the hand and designed to protect the arm and upper torso of the soldier in battle while permitting freedom of movement to maneuver and counterattack. Yahweh, however, is complete protection—a *magen* that surrounds the psalmist before and behind."[8]

Since the LORD is David's shield (3:3), he can say, "I will not fear the tens of thousands drawn up against me on every side" (3:6). Since the LORD is David's shield (144:2), he can pray, "Deliver me and rescue me from the hands of foreigners whose mouths are full of lies, whose right hands are deceitful" (144:11).

---

7. Kidner, *Psalms 1–72*, 219.
8. Wilson, *The New Application Commentary: Psalms—Volume 1*, 131.

Book 1 Pss 1–41	Book 2 Pss 42–72	Book 3 Pss 73–89	Book 4 Pss 90–106	Book 5 Pss 107–150
3:3; 7:10; 18:2, 30, 35; 28:7; 33:20; 35:2	47:9; 59:11	76:3; 84:9, 11; 89:18	? This term for shield does not appear in Book 4. This raises a few questions. Have there been times in your life when you have felt defenseless? Why? Where do you think God was during those times?	115:9, 10, 11; 119:114; 144:2

A second word for shield (GK 7558) is used three times in the Psalms (5:12; 35:2; 91:4). This word refers to the large shield (larger than the *magen*). Because of its size, the standing shield provided protection from many sides. Notice this emphasis in 5:12b: "you *surround* them [the righteous] with your favor as with a shield."[9]

Both terms are found at 35:2. In verse 1 David pleads with the LORD to "fight against those who fight against me." In verses two and three, God, the Warrior, is invited to join David dressed for battle: "take up shield (*magen*) and buckler . . . brandish spear and javelin against those who pursue me."

The Divine Warrior concept is commonly found in the Scriptures. As early as Exodus 15, this concept is found. Here Moses celebrates God's victory over the Egyptians. "The LORD is a warrior; the LORD is his name. Pharaoh's chariots and his army he has hurled into the sea" (15:3–4a). The Divine Warrior is credited with victory over the five kings who marched against Gibeon. "Surely the LORD was fighting for Israel"

---

9. For illustrations of these ancient shields, see Keel, *The Symbolism of the Ancient World: Ancient Near Eastern Iconography and the Book of Psalms*, 222-25.

(Josh 10:14). Psalm 24:8 succinctly says, "The LORD strong and mighty, the LORD mighty in battle" (see also 78:66).

Four of the verses above combine *magen* with a noun translated "help" (33:20; 115:9, 10, 11; GK 6469). These verses suggest that the LORD protects those in trouble, even in the throws of battle. God helps those who are poor in spirit, who trust and hope in him (notice this emphasis in these four verses).

This same noun for help also appears at 20:2; 70:5; 121:1, 2; 124:8 and 146:5. Speaking on behalf of future kings, David prays for help "when [they] are in distress" (20:2). David asks God for help because he is "poor and needy" (70:5). Since God is an ever-present help (121:1, 2), "he will watch over your life" (121:7). David thanks God for escape, a sure sign of the LORD's help (124:7–8). God helps (146:5) the oppressed, hungry, imprisoned, blind, bowed down, alien, fatherless, and the widow (146:7–9).

ROCK

In the book of Psalms two words are used for "Rock." The first (GK 6152) suggests a massive rock formation such as a cliff or mountainside. The second (GK 7446) refers to a single, large boulder, though there can be overlap with the first term.

The first term appears nine times in the Psalter. Four times the term is used metaphorically of the LORD/God. "The LORD is my rock" (18:2). "You are my rock" (31:3; 71:3). "I say to God my Rock" (42:9). The unyielding, indestructible firmness of a massive rock formation is a metaphor for refuge, a place of security from all trouble. Four are quite literal (78:16; 104:18; 137:9; 141:6). One bridges these two categories: "I waited patiently for the LORD; he turned to me and heard my cry. He lifted me out of the slimy pit, out of the mud and mire; he set my feet on a rock and gave me a firm place to stand" (40:1–2).

The second term appears twenty-four times. It is a metaphor for the faithfulness (reliability) of the LORD. He is the one on whom we rely. God is my/our Rock (18:2; 19:14; 28:1; 62:7; 78:35; 89:26; 92:15; 144:1), God alone (18:31; 62:2, 6). In the day of trouble, he is a reliable refuge (27:5; 31:2; 71:3; 94:22). When David prays, "Lead me to the rock that is higher than I" (61:2), he has in mind a place of security just out of his reach, but attainable when God pulls him upward. "Praise be to my

Rock!" (18:46). "Come, let us sing for joy to the LORD; let us shout aloud to the Rock of our salvation" (95:1).

This term can also be used in a literal sense. "He [God] split the rocks in the desert and gave them water as abundant as the seas" (78:15; see also 78:20; 81:16; 105:41; 114:8).

The NIV translation of 73:26b reads, "God is the strength of my heart." This half-verse literally says, "God is the rock of my heart." The psalmist suggests that even though the body may suffer pain or the heart endures sorrows (26a), God is his very life. Body and heart may even fail, but our life with God remains. In him alone we find and have life. "Earth has nothing I desire besides you" (73:25). If we rely on God, our Rock, we will find his ultimate refuge: glory itself (73:24).

These two nouns appear together in 71:3 (and also in 18:2). "Be my rock of refuge, to which I can always go; give the command to save me, for you are my rock and my fortress." The noun translated "refuge" (GK 5061) here occurs only four times in the Psalms (26:8; 68:5; 71:3; 91:9). The NIV translates this same word "dwelling" in 91:9 (as it does at 68:5). "If you make the Most High your dwelling—even the LORD, who is my refuge—then no harm will befall you, no disaster will come near your tent" (91:9–10). These two verses immediately precede the two that Satan quoted to Jesus when he tried to tempt him to throw himself down (Matt 4:6; Luke 4:10–11).

The expression "rock of refuge" also occurs at 31:2. A different noun for "refuge" is obviously used. This noun occurs nine times in Psalms (GK 5057). The noun conveys the sense of place or means of safety, protection. The NIV translates it "fortress" (28:8), "refuge" (31:2, 4), "stronghold" (27:1; 37:39; 43:2; 52:7)—all references to God—and "helmet" (60:7; 108:8).

FORTRESS

Thirteen times in the Psalter the LORD is referred to as a *mis-gav* (GK 5369). The NIV renders this word "refuge" (9:9), "stronghold" (9:9; 18:2; 144:2), and "fortress" (46:7, 11; 48:4; 59:9, 16, 17; 62:2, 6; 94:22). The Hebrew word suggests a secure height, a stronghold. The psalmists find the term useful because it suggests that God is a protected place, high and inaccessible, to which he can flee in times of encroaching trouble.

A related noun, "fortress" (GK 5181), is used six times of God (18:2; 31:2, 3; 71:3; 91:2; 144:2). This noun is translated "prison" at 66:11. This noun would have brought to David's mind his "wilderness sojourn," when Saul was pursuing him through the countryside and he was hiding in various safe places. The noun is used at 1 Sam 22:4, 5; 24:22; 2 Sam 5:17; 23:14 to describe David's hiding place and place of military operations (Cave of Adullam?). Jerusalem, the city of David, is twice (2 Sam 5:7, 9) referenced by this word.

On three occasions the Psalter says that "the world cannot be moved" (93:1; 96:10; 104:5). Because God is our refuge, the psalmists believe that we cannot be moved or shaken. "I have set the LORD always before me. Because he is at my right hand, I will not be shaken" (16:8; see also 15:5; 21:7; 30:6; 94:18; 112:6). "Those who trust in the LORD are like Mount Zion, which cannot be shaken but endures forever" (125:1). "He alone is my rock and my salvation; he is my fortress, I will never be shaken" (62:2, 6).

NEW TESTAMENT PARALLEL

Ephesians 6:10–18 speaks of the armor of God. This armor is necessary for the Christian to stand his or her ground against the Devil's evil schemes. The armor includes: belt of truth (6:14), breastplate of righteousness (6:14), feet fitted with the gospel of peace (6:15), shield of faith (6:16), helmet of salvation (6:17), sword of the Spirit (6:17), which is the Word of God, and prayer (6:18).

This word "shield" (GK 2599) appears only here in the New Testament. It is the long shield which covers the whole soldier. The shield of faith renders powerless the assault of the Devil. Peter exhorts Christians to resist the Devil, "standing firm in the faith" (1 Pet 5:9). The Devil may assault my health, my wealth, even life itself. But through faith in Christ I have a resurrected body (1 Cor 15:42–44), eternal treasures (1 Tim 6:19), and eternal life (John 3:16).

∽

"If you busy yourself in Psalms, you emerge knowing God." How does one busy oneself in a psalm or in a characteristic of God? You study, you meditate, you sing, and you pray.

MEDITATION

- In what or whom have you taken refuge? Why? How are you now taking refuge in God? What would your "refuge psalm" sound like?
- Do you have enemies? To what animal would you liken them? Why?
- Who or what is troubling you now? How is God helping you with these troubles?
- What does security mean to you? How do you find that in God?

MUSICAL REFLECTION

John Newton published "Amazing Grace" in 1779. His own life story bears elegant testimony to the profound words of this hymn. He spent many years at sea, surviving illnesses and violent storms. Spiritually he was the prodigal son of Luke 15. But the Lord's grace is amazing! The epitaph on Newton's tombstone speaks of the transformative power of grace. "John Newton, Clerk, once an infidel and libertine, a servant of slaves in Africa, was, by the rich mercy of our Lord and Savior, Jesus Christ, restored, pardoned, and appointed to preach the gospel he had long labored to destroy."

The Lord's grace was indeed a shield protecting John Newton from physical and spiritual death. What a gracious gift his life and this hymn became.

> Through many dangers, toils and snares,
> I have already come;
> 'Tis grace hath brought me safe thus far,
> And grace will lead me home.
> The Lord has promised good to me,
> His Word my hope secures;
> He will my Shield and Portion be,
> As long as life endures.

Between 1527 and 1529 Martin Luther wrote "A Mighty Fortress is Our God," a paraphrase of Psalm 46. The first and third verses are printed below. Note the certainty of the Devil's demise. Though he rage against us, we are safe, because our God is a mighty fortress.

> A mighty fortress is our God, a bulwark never failing;
> Our helper He, amid the flood of mortal ills prevailing:
> For still our ancient foe doth seek to work us woe;

His craft and power are great, and, armed with cruel hate,
On earth is not his equal.
And though this world, with devils filled, should threaten to undo us,
We will not fear, for God hath willed His truth to triumph through us:
The Prince of Darkness grim, we tremble not for him;
His rage we can endure, for lo, his doom is sure,
One little word shall fell him.

PRAYER

My God, the most righteous one, who is lifted high and sits enthroned, this world is dark and scary. I am attacked by evil on all sides. Externally, there are earthquake, fire, famine, political corruption, financial trouble, brutal murders, divorce, teenage pregnancy, drugs, alcohol, violence in the home, at the workplace, and at school. Within, there is depression, sadness, critical spirit, inferiority, low self-esteem, and unrest.

But you, O God, are not far off. You are here; you are my refuge, for I hide myself in you. Your goodness surrounds me. Your faithfulness, your love, and your holiness are round about me.

What can man or nature do to me when I am enclosed by you? My soul sings because you are good and there is no evil in you. My hope is renewed, for your loving kindness sustains me. You are my rock, for your words and actions are faithful. They are immovable and from everlasting to everlasting. Keep my eyes on you Lord.

Praise to you God. My heart glorifies you. My soul magnifies your holy name. I find rest and peace in you, Almighty God, Protector. Amen and Amen.

~

What are your song and your prayer?

7

God Is Deliverer

"I look for your deliverance, O LORD" (Genesis 49:18)

IN PSALM 18:2 DAVID refers to the LORD as "my Deliverer." He will do so again at 40:17, 70:5, and 144:2. David uses this term because the LORD has helped him evade or escape his enemies. David says the LORD is the one "who saves me from my enemies" (18:48).

This verbal root (GK 7117) appears nineteen times in the Psalter, making the idea a theme important to our consideration here. Many of these references focus on the psalmist's need or plight. "Rescue me from the wicked" (17:13). "You have delivered me from the attacks of the people" (18:43). "You will protect me from trouble" (32:7). "Rescue me from deceitful and wicked men" (43:1). "Deliver me, O my God, from the hand of the wicked, from the grasp of evil and cruel men" (71:4). "Rescue the weak and needy; deliver them from the hand of the wicked" (82:4).

| Book 1 | Book 2 | Book 3 | Book 4 | Book 5 |
Pss 1–41	Pss 42–72	Pss 73–89	Pss 90–106	Pss 107–150
17:13; 18:2, 43, 48; 22:4, 8; 31:1; 32:7; 37:40 (2x); 40:17	43:1; 56:7; 70:5; 71:2, 4	82:4	91:14	144:2

The verb "deliver" (GK 3828) occurs fifty-seven times in the Psalter. The majority of references speak of the Lord granting deliverance from real enemies. Since it is the Lord who delivers the community or an individual from distress to safety, he is the "Savior."

At the Red Sea the LORD delivered his people from the perilous prospect of the advancing Egyptians. "He saved them from the hand of the foe; from the hand of the enemy he redeemed them. The waters covered their adversaries; not one of them survived" (106:10–11; see also 106:21).

The LORD repeatedly delivers his people by granting victories on the battlefields. "I do not trust in my bow, my sword does not bring me victory; but you give us victory over our enemies, you put our adversaries to shame" (44:6–7; see also 44:3).

Not only does the LORD save the community, he saves the individuals that comprise that community. Whether it is the king or the anonymous commoner, it is the Lord who delivers. Since no king can be saved by the size of his army (33:16), the LORD must save or deliver the king of Israel from his enemies (20:6, 9). The LORD saves the upright in heart (7:10), the humble (18:27), those who are crushed in spirit (34:18), the needy who face death (72:13), the children of the needy (72:4), and the afflicted of the land (76:9).

The LORD saves by and because of his unfailing love (6:4; 31:16; 109:26); he saves by his name (54:1) and for his name's sake (106:8); and he saves by his right hand (17:7; 60:5; 98:1; 108:6; 138:7).

In times past, when God's people "cried to the LORD in their trouble," he saved them "from their distress" (107:13, 19). In light of the LORD's proven faithfulness, twenty-one times the psalmists use the imperative: "Save me!" (sixteen times) or "Save us!" (28:9; 60:5; 106:47; 108:6; 118:25).

At the end of Book Four (90–106), the people of God are in captivity, exiled because of their sin. Though that is the case, God's people still call to mind his past faithfulness and boldly plead: "Save us, O LORD our God, and gather us from the nations, that we may give thanks to your holy name and glory in your praise" (106:47).

The noun "deliverance, salvation" (GK 9591) occurs thirteen times in the Psalter. The salvation of the righteous comes only from the LORD (37:39). Accordingly, man cannot save or deliver (146:3). With God alone is victory, for the help ("salvation") of man is worthless (60:11; 108:12). The horse, which represents reliance on human power, is a "vain hope for deliverance" (33:17).

Since God alone is the one who saves (51:14) and gives victory (144:10), the psalmists long for God to save them from trouble (119:41,

81). The LORD is "My Savior" (38:22). When the psalmist experiences the LORD's salvation, the natural response is to exalt the LORD and to share the good news with others. "May all who seek you rejoice and be glad in you; may those who love your salvation always say, 'The LORD be exalted.'" (40:16). "My mouth will tell of your righteousness, of your salvation all day long, though I know not its measure" (71:15; see also 40:10).

A second noun for "salvation" (GK 3802) occurs forty-five times. Again, salvation comes only from the LORD. "He alone is my rock and my salvation" (62:2, 6). "My soul finds rest in God alone; my salvation comes from him" (62:1). "I am your salvation" (35:3; see also 3:8; 14:7; 53:6; 74:12). Since the LORD is Savior (68:19; 88:1; 89:26; 118:14, 21; 140:7), he is called upon to save or to deliver. "Awaken your might; come and save us" (80:2b). "I wait for your salvation" (119:166). "I long for your salvation" (119:174; see also 69:29; 106:4).

Again the psalmists feel compelled to testify to their experience. "Sing to the LORD, praise his name; proclaim his salvation day after day" (96:2; see also 9:14; 13:5–6; 35:9; 42:5, 11; 43:5; 70:4; 116:13).

The LORD gives his king great victories (18:50; 20:5; 21:1, 5; 28:8; 44:4; 118:15). He crowns the humble with salvation (149:4; see also 91:16). These wondrous acts help make his salvation known among all nations (67:2) and to the ends of the earth (98:2–3).

A second verb "deliver" (GK 5911) appears forty-five times. The LORD delivers from foes (18:17, 48; 31:15; 59:1–2; 142:6; 143:9) and fears (34:4); from troubles (34:17, 19; 54:7) and transgressions (39:8; 79:9), even murder itself (51:14); and from death (33:19; 56:13; 86:13). The urgency of these concerns prompts the psalmists to use the imperative eighteen times.

The LORD rescues or delivers the poor from those too strong for them (35:10). Through the king he delivers the needy who cry out (72:12). He delivers his faithful ones from the hand of the wicked (97:10). He delivers from the hands of oppressive foreigners (144:7, 11).

The verb "to redeem" (GK 7009) appears eleven times in the Psalter (twice in 107:2). The LORD as "my Redeemer" (19:14) occurs only once. At 69:18 "redeem" follows "come near and rescue me." The verb means "rescue" in 72:14. The great redemptive moment of the Old Testament, the Exodus, is remembered at 74:2; 77:15; 78:35; 106:10; and 107:2. The LORD redeems a life from the pit (103:4). "Deliver" and "redeem" are paired at 119:153–54.

The verb "to be merciful" (GK 2858) appears thirty-two times in the Psalms. Twenty-one times the psalmist uses the imperative, the command mode, to plead with the LORD for his mercy. In two verses, the plea for mercy is repeated. At 57:1 David pleads for mercy. He has just "fled from Saul into the cave." "Have mercy on me, O God, have mercy on me, for in you my soul takes refuge. I will take refuge in the shadow of your wings until the disaster has passed." At 123:3 the plea is communal. "Have mercy on us, O LORD, have mercy on us, for we have endured much contempt."

The verb is used three times in Psalm 119. Since the psalmist has committed himself to following the way of truth (v. 30), he desires to avoid deceitful ways (v. 29). Because the Law can unmask deceitful and fraudulent ways, the psalmist implores the LORD, "Be gracious/merciful to me through your law" (v. 29).

This same psalmist sought the LORD's face with all of his heart (v. 58). This pursuit involved obedience (vv. 57, 59, 60) and worship (v. 62). Would the LORD respond with blessing, as his word promised? The psalmist pleads, "Be gracious/merciful to me according to your promise" (v. 58).

At 119:132 the psalmist speaks of the "oppression of men." This deplorable situation exists because the "law is not obeyed" (v. 136). This has led to "streams of tears" (v. 136). And so the psalmist pleads, "Turn to me and have mercy on me, as you always do to those who love your name" (v. 132).

Book 1	Book 2	Book 3	Book 4	Book 5
Pss 1–41	Pss 42–72	Pss 73–89	Pss 90–106	Pss 107–150
4:1; 6:2; 9:13; 25:16; 26:11; 27:7; 30:8, 10; 31:9; 37:21, 26; 41:4, 10	51:1; 56:1; 57:1; 59:5; 67:1	86:3, 16	102:13, 14	109:12; 112:5; 119:29, 58, 132; 123:2, 3; 142:1

The noun "mercy, compassion" (GK 8171), which occurs eleven times, is related to the Hebrew word for "womb." The word suggests, then, a love as intense as a mother's love for her child. Because of God's great mercy (25:6), David can plead, "Remember not the sins of my youth and my rebellious ways" (25:7; see also 51:1; 79:8; 103:3–4). Because of God's great mercy (69:16), David and others can plead for rescue (69:18), for help (77:1, 9; see also 106:46), for protection (40:11), and for life itself (119:77, 156). "The LORD is good to all; he has compassion on all he has made" (145:9). The adjective "compassionate" is used five times of God (78:38; 86:15; 103:8; 111:4; 145:8) and once of man (112:4). The corresponding verb, "have compassion, love," is used three times of God (102:13; 103:13; 116:5) and once of man (18:1). "The LORD is gracious and righteous; our God is full of compassion" (116:5).[1]

The term "horn" (GK 7967) is found thirteen times in the Psalter. The animal horn is a symbol of power, strength, and victory. The term may be used to signify a king (89:17; 132:17; 148:14), to symbolize the brutish strength of the enemy (22:21; 75:4, 5, 10) or the saving strength of God (18:2), or the blessing of strength/dignity (89:24; 92:10; 112:9). Psalm 118:27 speaks of the horns of the altar—the projections of the four corner posts. They were symbols of refuge (1 Kings 1:50; 2:28) or atonement (Exod 30:10). "To envision Yahweh as the psalmist's 'horn,'" writes Wilson, "is to understand that Yahweh is the source of power and strength that ensures the psalmist's ultimate victory against his foes."[2]

The verb "keep, watch, guard" (GK 9068) appears seventy-one times in the Psalter, twenty-one times alone in Psalm 119, where it typically means "to obey" (see, for example, 119:44).

When God is the subject of the verb, two primary usages are evident. First, God watches over his people. "The LORD watches over all who love him, but the wicked he will destroy" (145:20; see also 34:19–20; 41:2; 97:10; 116:6; 127:1). Six times in Psalm 121 this idea is voiced (vv. 3, 4, 5, 7 [twice], 8). But the LORD does watch over the alien (146:9). Watching, of course, is more than just observation, it is decisive action. This leads to the second point. Second, often with an imperative (the command mode) on their lips, God's people cry out to him, asking for protection. "Keep me safe, O God, for in you I take refuge" (16:1; see also 12:7). "Guard my life and rescue me; let me not be put to shame, for I take refuge in you" (25:20). "Guard my life, for I am devoted to you. You are my God; save your servant who trusts in you" (86:2; see also 91:11). "Keep me, O LORD, from the hands of the wicked" (140:4; see also 141:9).

---

1. Three times in the Psalms, the image of God as father is used. He is "a father to the fatherless" (68:5) and a father to Israel's reigning king (89:26). "As a father has compassion on his children, so the LORD has compassion on those who fear him" (103:13).

2. Wilson, *Psalms Volume 1*, 339.

The LORD maintains his watch forever. "For the LORD loves the just and will not forsake his faithful ones. They will be protected forever, but the offspring of the wicked will be cut off" (37:28; see also 89:28; 146:6).

Those whom the LORD has delivered have waited upon him. The verb "to wait for, hope for" (GK 3498) appears nineteen times. The LORD delights in those who have put their hope in him (31:24; 33:22; 38:15; 42:5, 11; 43:5; 69:3; 130:7; 131:3), in his love (33:18; 147:11), or in his word (119:43, 49, 74, 81, 114, 147; 130:5). This waiting is no passive acceptance of circumstances though. "I rise before dawn and cry for help" (119:147). "My soul faints with longing" (119:81). "I am worn out calling for help; my throat is parched" (69:3). "Be strong" (31:24). "In the Psalms," writes Kraus, "'to wait' means not giving up, not growing tired, not surrendering to overwhelming grief, but persevering expectantly."[3] Trouble and suffering have no earthly end, and so, we wait on the LORD.

A second verb with similar meaning occurs seventeen times (GK 7747). David waited patiently for the LORD (40:1), but he had to wait in the slimy pit, in the mud and mire (40:2). Another psalmist cries out of the depths to the LORD (130:1), while waiting upon the LORD (130:5). Those who hope in or wait for the LORD (25:5, 21; 27:14; 39:7; 52:9) will never be put to shame (25:3; 69:6), because they have surrendered themselves to trusting in God.

NEW TESTAMENT PARALLEL

The word Savior (GK 5400) occurs twenty-four times in the New Testament. The title is used exclusively for either God (Luke 1:47; 1 Tim 1:1; 2:3; 4:10; Titus 1:3; 2:10; Jude 25) or for Jesus Christ (Luke 2:11; Titus 1:4; 2 Pet 1:1, 11; 2:20; 3:2, 18). Jesus is the Savior or deliverer of Israel (Acts 5:31; 13:23), the Samaritans (John 4:42), the church (Eph 5:23), indeed, the world (1 John 4:14). The salvation or deliverance Jesus offers is not political. He does not deliver, for example, Israel from Roman rule and oppression. He saves or delivers people from sin and death. With respect to sin, Paul writes of our great God and Savior, Jesus Christ, "who gave himself for us to redeem us from all wickedness and to purify for himself a people that are his very own, eager to do what is good" (Titus 2:14; see also 3:4–7). With respect to death, Paul writes to Timothy, "This

---

3. Kraus, *Theology of the Psalms*, 158.

grace was given us in Christ Jesus before the beginning of time, but it has now been revealed through the appearing of our Savior, Christ Jesus, who has destroyed death and has brought life and immortality to light through the gospel" (2 Tim 1:9b–10).

The truth of a believer's deliverance from sin and death is both present reality and future hope. Even though our salvation has already been actualized, it has a future consummation. Paul writes of this in his letter to the Philippians: "But our citizenship is in heaven. And we eagerly await a Savior from there, the Lord Jesus Christ, who, by the power that enables him to bring everything under his control, will transform our lowly bodies so that they will be like his glorious body" (3:20–21).

The verb "to show mercy" (GK 1796) occurs twenty-eight times in the New Testament. Upon request—"have mercy"—Jesus showed mercy by granting sight to blind Bartimaeus (Mark 10:47, 48, 52; Luke 18:38–39, 42–43; Matt 20:30, 31, 34), by granting sight to two blind men (Matt 9:27, 30), by healing a child suffering greatly with seizures (Matt 17:15, 18), by healing ten men with leprosy (Luke 17:13, 14), by casting out demons from a man of the Gerasenes (Mark 5:19), and by casting out a demon from a little girl (Matt 15:22, 28).

God showed mercy to the Gentiles by grafting them into his kingdom through Jesus (Rom 11:30). Gentile inclusion has led and will lead to the return of Jews to that same kingdom (Rom 11:31). From Paul's vantage point, Gentiles were on the outside looking in due to their own disobedience, and Jews are now on the outside looking in for the same reason. Paul concludes, "For God has bound all men over to disobedience so that he may have mercy on them all" (Rom 11:32).

God showed mercy to Epaphroditus by healing him from a life-threatening illness (Phil 2:27). Paul saw the healing as an act of God's mercy upon himself as well, "to spare me sorrow upon sorrow." Paul was no stranger to God's mercy: "Even though I was once a blasphemer and a persecutor and a violent man, I was shown mercy because I acted in ignorance and unbelief" (1 Tim 1:13; see also 1:16).

Those who have been shown mercy are merciful people (Matt 5:7), at least, should be (Matt 18:33). If God is merciful, and he is (Rom 9:15, 18; 1 Pet 2:10), then His people must show mercy. Paul saw God's mercy as the compelling reason for his own ministry (2 Cor 4:1).

"If you busy yourself in Psalms, you emerge knowing God." How does one busy oneself in a psalm or in a characteristic of God? You study, you meditate, you sing, and you pray.

MEDITATION

- Have there been times in your life when, like Book 1, your need for deliverance was constant? When? Why?
- Reflect on the Lord's proven faithfulness in your life. When did you last cry out, "Save me!"?
- Have there been seasons, like Books 3 and 4, when you have not been overly mindful of the Lord's mercy? Why?
- How are you now relying on the Lord's strength?
- Have you surrendered to trusting in God? What may be preventing this surrender?
- When did you last thank Jesus for his mercy? What was the occasion?

Two primary verbs for "seek" (GK 1335 and 2011) are used in the Psalter. Please notice below two vital truths. First, we are to seek him! Second, the one who seeks the LORD, our Deliverer, is blessed in countless ways.

to seek (GK 1335)	to seek (GK 2011)
"One thing I ask of the LORD, this is what I seek: that I may dwell in the house of the LORD all the days of my life" (27:4)	"You, LORD, have never forsaken those who seek you" (9:10)
"Your face, LORD, I will seek" (27:8). "Seek his face always" (105:4)	"They who seek the LORD will praise him" (22:26)
"Seek peace and pursue it" (34:14)	"He will receive blessing from the LORD and vindication from God his Savior. Such is the generation of those who seek him, who seek your face, O God of Jacob" (24:5–6)

to seek (GK 1335)	to seek (GK 2011)
"May all who seek you rejoice and be glad in you" (40:16; 70:4; see also 105:3)	"I sought the LORD and he answered me" (34:4)
	"Those who seek the LORD lack no good thing" (34:10)
	"You who seek God, may your hearts live!" (69:32)
	"Seek his face always" (105:4)
	"Blessed are they who keep his statutes and seek him with all their heart" (119:2; see also 119:10, 45, 94, 155)

Have you wholeheartedly been seeking the Lord? Who or what has been or is now in the way? How has the Lord blessed your search?

MUSICAL REFLECTION

In 1875 American hymn writer Philip P. Bliss (1838–1876) wrote "Hallelujah, What A Saviour!"

> Man of Sorrows! what a name
> For the Son of God, Who came
> Ruined sinners to reclaim.
> Hallelujah! What a Savior!
>
> Bearing shame and scoffing rude,
> In my place condemned He stood;
> Sealed my pardon with His blood.
> Hallelujah! What a Savior!
>
> Guilty, vile, and helpless we;
> Spotless Lamb of God was He;
> "Full atonement!" can it be?
> Hallelujah! What a Savior!
>
> Lifted up was He to die;
> "It is finished!" was His cry;
> Now in heav'n exalted high.
> Hallelujah! What a Savior!
>
> When He comes, our glorious King,
> All His ransomed home to bring,
> Then anew His song we'll sing:
> Hallelujah! What a Savior!

PRAYER

Lord, have mercy (*Kyrie eleison*). Christ, have mercy (*Christe eleison*). Lord, have mercy (*Kyrie eleison*). Lord, Son of David, have mercy on us (Matt 20:30, 31). Jesus, son of David, have mercy on me (Mark 10:47). God, have mercy on me, a sinner (Luke 18:13). Amen.

O Mighty God and Savior, you are full of mercy and compassion. Because of your unfailing love, you have saved me. When I was crushed in spirit, you made me whole. When I faced death, you comforted me. When I was wounded by my enemies, you healed me. When I was frightened, you reassured me. When I was in the pit of confusion and depression, you lifted me out and placed my feet on secure ground—the foundation of everlasting love.

Father, for you to be my deliverer, I must be in trouble. I need your help. It means that I am hurt or in great danger of being hurt. Father, I don't like pain. I don't like hurting. Why does there have to be any sorrow, any trouble? I know there is free will, and I know that you said that there would be trouble in this world. Your response to trouble, my trouble, is, "I have overcome." I am so grateful.

It is you who have overcome sorrow, disease, and death, and we are saved by you. I acknowledge that the saving is not always immediately obvious. We can become weary and wasted by the spiritual war we wage. Yet, even if this life is threatened and death comes, even then you have delivered us. Thank you, God. You are painfully aware of my struggles. Thank you for being so powerful that you have lifted me out of the pit. I think it fitting that the word for *compassion* is related to the word for *womb*. The intimate, passionate, possessive, and protective love of a mother for her unborn child is a beautiful image for understanding your love for me. Have mercy on me, your child. Amen.

What are your song and your prayer?

8

God Is Great, Good, and Loving

"Great is the LORD and most worthy of praise;
his greatness no one can fathom" (Psalm 145:3)

GREAT

The adjective "great" (GK 1524) and derived nouns are reserved almost exclusively in the Psalter for God. Twenty-five of the thirty-four total occurrences refer to God (74 percent).

The nine exceptions shall detain us only for a brief time. Psalm 21:5 uses the adjective for the glory of the king in Israel (David), but this is true only because of the military victories God has given. The *vast* sea (104:25), its inhabitants ("living things both *large* and small"), and the great lights (136:7) are counted among the works of God. It is God who struck down great kings (136:17) as his people entered their promised land. The LORD will bless those who fear him—small and great alike (115:13). The adjective is used at 12:4 for a *boastful* tongue and again at 131:1 for great matters. A derived noun "honor" is found at 71:21.

The LORD is great! "He determines the number of the stars and calls them each by name. Great is our Lord and mighty in power; his understanding has no limit" (147:4–5). "Great is the LORD, and most worthy of praise" (48:1; 96:4). His name is great and awesome (99:3). His name is great in Israel (76:1). The name in ancient culture was synonymous with an individual's (human or divine) character. God's revelation of His character is knowable—He is great!

God's love is great. His love reaches to the heavens (57:10). In fact, God's great love is higher than the heavens (108:4). God's great love is also personal and present—"I will praise you, O LORD my God, with all my heart; I will glorify your name forever. For great is your love toward me; you have delivered my soul from the depths of the grave" (86:12-13). Psalm 145:8 best summarizes this divine attribute: "The LORD is gracious and compassionate, slow to anger and rich (great) in love."

God's sovereignty is great. This reality is expressed through the vocabulary of kingship (47:2; 95:3). His reign is spatially universal: "For the LORD is the great God, the great king above all gods. In his hand are the depths of the earth, and the mountain peaks belong to him. The sea is his, for he made it, and his hands formed the dry land" (95:3-5). "How awesome is the LORD Most high, the great king over all the earth!" (47:2; see also 7-9).

God is praised for the great things he has done: creation (136:4), deliverance from Egypt (106:21), providence and redemption (111:2). The psalmist writes, "I will proclaim your great deeds" (145:6).

God's glory is great. "May all the kings of the earth praise you, O LORD, when they hear the words of your mouth. May they sing of the ways of the LORD, for the glory of the LORD is great" (138:4-5). The glorious strength ("greatness") of God's arm is appealed to for self-preservation (79:11).

God's greatness is compared to that of other nations (99:2: "He is exalted over all the nations") and to that of other gods (71:19; 77:13; 95:3; 135:5 ["our LORD is greater than all gods"]). Psalm 86:10 is the summation of the matter: "For you are great and do marvelous deeds, you alone are God."

Even though the totality of His greatness is beyond human comprehension (145:3), we are still encouraged to "praise him for his surpassing greatness" (150:2). The LORD is great!

Psalm 147

This psalm's length is defined by the beginning and ending imperative, "Praise the LORD." The psalm's depth is sounded by three summons to praise (vv. 1, 7, 12), forming three units: vv. 1-6, 7-11, and 12-20.

Verse 4 reminds us that God's greatness extends throughout the cosmos—"He determines the number of the stars and calls them each by name." The wrong inference to draw from this transcendence is that He is too great to care. The right inference is that He is too great to fail His people. Listen to verse 3: "He heals the brokenhearted and binds up their wounds."

In verses 8–9, God's attention to the life cycle, from the clouds that supply the rainfall to the food for the cattle, suggests the greatness of God's provision for his creation. His provision is meant to foster in us a spirit of humility and trust. "The LORD delights in those who fear him, who put their hope in his unfailing love" (v. 11).

God has revealed the greatness of His word (commanding—verse 15—and compelling) to His people alone. "He has revealed his word to Jacob, his laws and decrees to Israel. He has done this for no other nation; they do not know his laws" (vv. 19–20).

GOOD

The adjective "good" (GK 3202) appears thirty-six times in the Psalter. The LORD is good (100:5; 106:1; 107:1; 118:1, 29; 119:68; 135:3; 136:1), as is his spirit (143:10) and his words (119:39). "Good and upright is the LORD" (25:8). "Taste and see that the LORD is good" (34:8). "The LORD is good to all; he has compassion on all he has made" (145:9). "Your name is good" (52:9; 54:6). His love is good (69:16). "You are forgiving and good, O LORD, abounding in love to all who call to you" (86:5). Because of the goodness of God's love, David can plead for deliverance (109:21). Since God is good to Israel (73:1), it is good to be near God (73:28). "It is good to praise the LORD" (92:1). "How good it is to sing praises to our God, how pleasant and fitting to praise him" (147:1).

The Hebrew noun often translated "goodness" (GK 3206) appears seven times in the Psalter. Convinced that the LORD will deliver him from his enemies, David can say, "I will see the goodness of the LORD in the land of the living" (27:13). That goodness, which is bestowed on those who take refuge in him, is great (31:19) and abundant (145:7). The LORD can teach good judgment (119:66) because he is good (25:7). The noun is translated "prosperity" at 128:5.

Psalm 65:4 says, "Blessed are those you choose and bring near to live in your courts! We are filled with the good things of your house, of your holy temple." The reference to "courts" might suggest the author is a priest. But since the author is David, we must take these words as metaphor for experiencing the nearness of God. If we draw near to God in his house, then we will experience his luxuriant hospitality: "We are filled with the good things" of his house! The content of this psalm—delighting in God as Forgiver (vv. 1–3), Creator (vv. 5–8), and Provider (vv. 9–13)—is just one of those "good things."

Another of those good things is an appreciation of the land's "bounty" (65:11). This word "bounty" is a dynamic translation of another Hebrew noun for "good things, good" (GK 3208). This noun appears only twice more in the Psalter. It is translated "bounty" again at 68:10. At 16:2 David can say that the LORD is his "highest good" (literally, "You are my good—there is none above you"). Psalm 73:25 provides sublime commentary here. "Whom have I in heaven but you? And earth has nothing I desire besides you."

A third noun, translated "a good thing, benefit, welfare" (GK 3202), appears twenty-nine times. Only the LORD can "show us any good" (4:6). The "LORD will indeed give what is good, and our land will yield its harvest" (85:12; see also 107:9). The LORD showers "rich" blessings on his anointed (21:3). The LORD's goodness and love will follow the king all the days of his life (23:6). The LORD's help and comfort are signs of goodness to the king (86:17). The God-fearer will enjoy "prosperity" (25:13; 106:5; 122:9; 128:2) and many good days (34:12), lacking no good thing (34:10; 84:11). The LORD satisfies the soul's desire with good things (103:5). The creatures of the earth are satisfied with good things, that is, their food (104:28). The moral atheist (the one who lives as if there were no god) does not do what is good (14:1, 3; 53:1, 3), repaying evil for good (35:12; 38:20; 52:3; 109:5). Since the LORD does good (119:65, 122), his will for us, of course, is to do what is good (34:14; 37:3, 27; 39:2).

Four men in the Old Testament bear the name Tobijah, which means "the LORD is my good" (2 Chr 17:8; Neh 2:10; 7:62; Zech 6:10).

LOVING

In Psalms the term *hesed* (GK 2876) is used 127 times (245 times in the entire Old Testament). The NIV often translates this term as "love" or "unfailing love." Thirty-six times the Psalter declares that His love endures forever (89:2; 100:5; 106:1; 107:1; 118:1–4, 29; 136:1–26; 138:8; see also 25:6; 89:28; 103:17). His love extends to the heavens (36:5; 57:10). In fact, David can say that His love is "higher than the heavens" (108:4). His love fills the earth (33:5; 119:64).

This great love (17:7; 86:13; 89:49; 103:11; 117:2), which is better than life (63:3), is given to Israel (98:3) and its kings (18:50; 21:7; 61:7; 89:24, 33). The LORD's abounding love (86:5, 15; 103:8; 145:8) is the basis for Israel's trust (13:5; 21:7; 32:10; 52:8; 143:8) and hope (33:18, 22; 130:7; 147:11).

Those who pray appeal to the LORD's love: "save me because of your unfailing love" (6:4b; 31:16; see also 57:3; 109:26); "according to your love remember me" (25:7); "may your love and your truth always protect me" (40:11); "redeem us because of your unfailing love" (44:26); "have mercy on me, O God, according to your unfailing love" (51:1); "in your great love, O God, answer me with your sure salvation" (69:13b; see also 69:16); "satisfy us in the morning with your unfailing love" (90:14); "out of the goodness of your love, deliver me" (109:21b); "may your unfailing love be my comfort" (119:76); "preserve my life according to your love" (119:88a, 159; see also 119:149); "deal with your servant according to your love" (119:124); "in your unfailing love, silence my enemies" (143:12a).

This love compels worship (5:7) and is often the subject of that worship. "Let them give thanks to the LORD for his unfailing love" (107:8, 15, 21, 31). God's people consider (107:43b) and meditate on this love (48:9); through song (59:16; 89:1; 101:1) and proclamation (40:10; 92:2), we praise God for this love (138:2). "Not to us, O LORD, not to us but to your name be the glory, because of your love and faithfulness" (115:1). "I will be glad and rejoice in your love" (31:7a; see also 31:21).

We are fully enveloped by this love. "Your love is ever before me, and I walk continually in your truth" (26:3; see also 59:10; 89:14b). This love will pursue us all the days of our lives (23:6).

The ancient pagans may have confused this love with a romanticism or eroticism. No, this love is grounded in God's commitment to a holy relationship. We could translate *hesed* as "covenant loyalty." Our God is not a fertility god; he is a God of covenant fidelity. Gerald Wilson has said it well: "We trust God because He has shown and continues to show that he is committed to us absolutely. He loves us in that he is willing to suffer our anger and rejection, our sin and rebellion, and still accomplish his will and purpose for us—to woo us to himself in a restored relationship."[1]

Only twice in the Psalms is God the subject of the common verb "hate" (GK 8533). He "hates all who do wrong" (5:5), and his soul hates "the wicked and those who love violence" (11:5).

The term "covenant" (GK 1382) occurs twenty-one times. All but two (55:20; 83:5) refer to the unique relationship the LORD and Israel shared, a relationship initiated in God's grace and experienced by Israel

---

1. Wilson, *Psalms Volume 1*, 856–857.

through obedience and worship (50:5). This relationship began with a promise made to the patriarchs: Abraham, Isaac, and Jacob. "He remembers his covenant forever, the word he commanded, for a thousand generations, the covenant he made with Abraham, the oath he swore to Isaac. He confirmed it to Jacob as a decree, to Israel as an everlasting covenant" (105:8–10). Psalm 89:3–4 speaks to God's ongoing commitment to his people, focused now in the promise made to David. "You said, 'I have made a covenant with my chosen one, I have sworn to David my servant. I will establish your line forever and make your throne firm through all generations'" (see also 89:34–35; 132:11–12).

Psalm 25:10 speaks to Israel's obedience. "All the ways of the LORD are loving and faithful for those who keep the demands of his covenant." Unfortunately, Israel did not always keep the demands of the covenant (78:10, 37).

Psalm 103:17–18 offers a beautiful summation of this gracious relationship. "But from everlasting to everlasting the LORD's love is with those who fear him, and his righteousness with their children's children—with those who keep his covenant and remember to obey his precepts."

Forever

In the Psalter the following are true "forever." The LORD reigns or rules forever (9:7; 66:7; 146:10). In other words, he is king forever (10:16; 29:10; 102:12; see also 45:6). His kingdom is forever (145:13). His love endures or stands firm forever (25:6; 89:2; 100:5; 103:17; 106:1; 107:1; 118:1, 2, 3, 4, 29; 136:1–26; 138:8). His faithfulness is eternal (117:2; 146:6), as is his righteousness (111:3; 119:142). He is exalted forever (92:8). "Praise be to the LORD from everlasting to everlasting" (41:13; see also 72:19; 79:13; 89:52; 106:48; 111:10; 113:2). He is from all eternity (93:2); "from eternity to eternity you are God" (90:2). His name endures forever (135:13). His word is eternal (119:89; see also 119:152, 160), forever right (119:144), and steadfast for ever and ever (111:8). The LORD forever protects his people (37:28; 55:22; 125:2). The plans of the LORD stand firm forever (33:11).

NEW TESTAMENT PARALLEL

The Creator (Rom 1:25; 1 Tim 6:16) and Christ (Rom 9:5; 2 Cor 11:31) are forever praised. To God "be the glory forever!" (Rom 11:36). To Jesus "be glory both now and forever" (2 Pet 3:18). "To the only wise God be glory forever through Jesus Christ!" (Rom 16:27).

Quoting Isaiah 40:6–8, Peter affirms that the "word of the Lord stands forever" (1 Pet 1:25; see also 1:23; 2 John 2).

Because Jesus lives forever (Heb 7:24), he exercises a permanent priesthood. The Lord God swore by oath concerning the priesthood of Jesus: "You are a priest forever" (Heb 5:6; 6:20; 7:17, 21, 28). Jesus' priesthood is eternal, as is his reign (Luke 1:33) and person (Heb 13:8).

After Jesus ascended to the right hand of the Father, he sent the Spirit, who would bear witness to mankind concerning the lordship of Jesus. The Holy Spirit, the Spirit of truth, another Counselor, will be with the believer and the believing community forever (John 14:16).

The man or woman who believes in Jesus (John 6:51, 58) and does the will of God will live forever (1 John 2:17). At the second coming of Christ, we will be with the Lord forever (1 Thess 4:17; see also 1 Cor 9:25), proof of the perfection Jesus has been working in us (Heb 10:14).

Blackest darkness has been reserved forever, however, for false teachers (Jude 13).

∼

"If you busy yourself in Psalms, you emerge knowing God." How does one busy oneself in a psalm or in a characteristic of God? You study, you meditate, you sing, and you pray.

MEDITATION

- How do you understand the terms *great* and *good*?
- What similar words help you capture the essence of the ideas presented here in the Psalms?
- God's love is foundational. You understand this intellectually, but have you experienced His love?
- When you contemplate the great acts of God throughout history, do you notice that your point of view changes?
- When you look through the lens of God, what do you learn about him and yourself?

God Is Great, Good, and Loving

MUSICAL REFLECTION

In 1747 Charles Wesley (1707–1788) wrote one of his 6,500 hymns, "Love Divine, All Loves Excelling."

> Love divine, all loves excelling, joy of heav'n, to earth come down; fix in us Thy humble dwelling; all Thy faithful mercies crown. Jesus, Thou art all compassion; pure, unbounded love Thou art; visit us with Thy salvation; enter ev'ry trembling heart.
>
> Breathe, O breathe Thy loving Spirit into ev'ry troubled breast! Let us all in Thee inherit; let us find that second rest. Take away our bent to sinning, Alpha and Omega be; end of faith, as its beginning, set our hearts at liberty.
>
> Come, almighty to deliver, let us all Thy life receive; suddenly return, and never, nevermore Thy temples leave. Thee we would be always blessing, serve Thee as Thy hosts above, pray and praise Thee without ceasing, glory in Thy perfect love.
>
> Finish then Thy new creation; pure and spotless let us be; let us see Thy great salvation perfectly restored in Thee. Changed from glory into glory, till in heav'n we take our place, till we cast our crowns before Thee, lost in wonder, love and praise.

PRAYER

O great and good God, you overwhelm me. You created the stars and call them out by name. You created the seas and you hold them in the palm of your hand.

Your glory, sovereignty, and holiness are like none other. It surpasses all that has existed or will exist. And yet, and yet, your love for me and compassion for my issues are everlasting. Your love for me is higher than the stars. Your love protects me; your love saves me; your love satisfies me; your love delivers me; and your love preserves me. You deal with me in love and your love comforts me.

O great God, you are indeed God alone. Amen.

What are your song and your prayer?

9

God Is Righteous

> "For the LORD is righteous, he loves righteous deeds;
> the upright shall behold his face" (Psalm 11:7)

THE TERM "RIGHTEOUS" OCCURS fifty-two times in the Psalter. Surprisingly, this adjective (GK 7404) is used of the LORD/God only seven times. God/the LORD is righteous (7:9; 11:7; 116:5; 119:137; 129:4). Indeed, "he is righteous in all his ways" (145:17). The only specific role or function of God, however, qualified by this adjective is that of judge (7:11). The starting point of our understanding of this term is God's work of judging. The LORD is righteous because he judges righteously. This means, according to Kraus, "the bringing of assistance, deliverance, and loyalty to those who are victims of injustice, persecution, and false accusations."[1]

The noun "righteousness" (GK 7407) occurs thirty-four times in the Psalter. All but four (106:3, 31; 112:3, 9) are theologically instructive. "The righteousness of Yahweh is the perfection of the manner in which he sees through everything, evaluates, judges, and saves. It is the perfection of the one who, true to his responsibilities to the community, helps all who are oppressed, falsely accused, persecuted, or suffering, and reveals himself as their deliverer."[2]

Because the LORD is righteous, he loves righteousness (33:5) or justice (11:7). He has done what is just and right (99:4). He "works vindication and justice for all who are oppressed" (103:6). Listen to the oppressed cry out for righteousness: "Lead me, O LORD, in thy righteousness because of my enemies" (5:8). "In thee, O LORD, do I seek

---

1. Kraus, *Theology of the Psalms*, 43.
2. Ibid.

refuge; let me never be put to shame; in thy righteousness deliver me" (31:1). "O continue thy steadfast love to those who know thee, and thy righteousness to the upright of heart!" (36:10). "In thy righteousness deliver me and rescue me" (71:2). "Hear my prayer, O LORD; give ear to my supplications! In thy faithfulness answer me, in thy righteousness!" (143:1). "For thy name's sake, O LORD, preserve my life! In thy righteousness, bring me out of trouble!" (143:11; see also 119:40).

Those whom the LORD has saved will forever join their voices in a chorus of praise. "My mouth will tell of thy righteous acts, of thy deeds of salvation all the day, for their number is past my knowledge" (71:15; see also 22:31; 40:10; 51:15; 71:16, 24; 88:12; 89:16; 145:7).

The LORD's righteousness "reaches the high heavens" (71:19) and endures forever (111:3; 119:42). It is likened to the mighty mountains (36:6; see also 72:3). It is cherished by one generation (24:5–6) and desired for the next (72:1; 103:17). It is a matter of public record, even for the nations. "The LORD has made known his victory, he has revealed his vindication in the sight of the nations" (98:2).

The uniqueness of the LORD—who is like you?—is evident in his righteousness. "O LORD, who is like thee, thou who deliverest the weak from him who is too strong for him, the weak and needy from him who despoils him?" (35:10). "Thy power and thy righteousness, O God, reach the high heavens. Thou who hast done great things, O God, who is like thee?" (71:19; see also 86:8; 89:8).

The noun "firmness, faithfulness, truth" (GK 622) is derived from the verb "confirm, support" and has the connotations of "firm, reliable, valid, and true." This noun occurs thirty-seven times in the Psalter. Every occurrence, save two (15:2; 45:4), is theologically instructive.

The LORD is a faithful God, reliable in deed and in word. Psalm 31:5 reads, "Into thy hand I commit my spirit; thou hast redeemed me, O LORD, faithful God." Since the saving faithfulness of the LORD is constant and true, David can appeal to and rely on the LORD's help. "I am the talk of those who sit in the gate, and the drunkards make songs about me. But as for me, my prayer is to thee, O LORD. At an acceptable time, O God, in the abundance of thy steadfast love answer me" (69:12–13). All the works of His hands are faithful (25:10; 111:7).

Just as the deeds of the LORD are reliable and true, so are his words. "Thy law is true" (119:142); "all thy commandments are true" (119:151); "the sum of thy word is truth; and every one of thy righteous ordinances endure for ever" (119:160; see also 19:9; 119:43). When he swears an oath or pronounces a promise, those words are sure to be fulfilled (132:11).

Since the LORD "keeps faith for ever" (146:6; see also 117:2) and the works of his hands are "established for ever and ever" (111:8), he is our ever-present protection. "Let thy steadfast love and thy faithfulness ever preserve me!" (40:11b; see also 61:7). "His faithfulness is a shield and buckler" (91:4; see also 57:3). He is also our ever-present basis for expectant justice. "He will requite my enemies with evil; in thy faithfulness put an end to them" (54:5).

Because the LORD and his word are true and reliable (89:14), wisdom dictates that we follow them! David has it right when he writes, "I walk continually in your truth" (26:3, NIV). David again says, "Teach me thy way, O LORD, that I may walk in thy truth" (86:11). Wisdom also dictates that they be our guide! "Make me to know thy ways, O LORD; teach me thy paths. Lead me in thy truth, and teach me" (25:4–5a; see also 43:3; 145:18). Wisdom also demands that His truth wells up in both life (51:6; see also 40:10; 85:9–12) and worship (30:9; 71:22; 115:1; 138:2).

The LORD is forever true to his character—He is permanent fidelity. The LORD abounds in faithfulness (86:15). In fact his faithfulness reaches to the skies (57:10; 108:4). Contrast this with the capricious nature of the ancient gods.

The noun *emunah*, "faithfulness" (GK 575), also testifies to the LORD's constancy and reliability. There is nothing arbitrary in the LORD's character and commitment to Israel (98:3). "In his freedom he is the one who is reliable and true to his community."[3] This noun occurs twenty-two times.

Faithfulness surrounds the LORD (89:8). This reliability reaches to the skies (36:5), even to heaven itself (89:2, 5). This reliability or faithfulness marks all of time (92:2) and thus "endures for ever" (100:5; 119:90).

The LORD is "faithful in all he does" (33:4, NIV). His "steadfast love" will accompany the anointed kings of Israel (89:24). This love will prompt them to pray for mercy and deliverance (143:1), and then to enjoy the security or safety found in it (37:3). This love will provide a context for understanding affliction (119:75). He will be true to truth in judgment (96:13).

---

3. Ibid., 45.

God Is Righteous

The LORD is also faithful and truthful in all he says. He will be true to a promise, such as the promise made to David (89:49). "I will not remove from him my steadfast love, or be false to my faithfulness" (89:33). All the LORD's commands are trustworthy (119:86); they are fully trustworthy (119:138; see also 119:30).

Not surprisingly, the LORD's faithfulness inspires worship and proclamation. "I will sing of thy steadfast love, O LORD, for ever; with my mouth I will proclaim thy faithfulness to all generations" (89:1). "I have spoken of thy faithfulness and thy salvation. I have not concealed thy steadfast love and thy faithfulness from the great congregation" (40:10; see also 88:11).

The verb "judge, govern" (GK 9149) occurs thirty-two times in the Psalter. Three of these refer to rulers of the earth (2:10; 141:6; 148:11). Four times David asks the LORD for vindication (= "judge me" [7:8; 26:1; 35:24; 43:1]). Four times the act of judging leads to a defense of the oppressed. God may be the judge (10:18), or an Israelite king may be the judge (72:4; 82:2, 3).

God sits as judge (50:6) over his covenant people (50:5) and over the nations of this earth (9:19; 58:11; 82:8). When any person or people are brought to trial in the court of God, there is a finding of sin. David, for example, fully aware of his sin in the affair with Bathsheba, says of God, "thou art justified in thy sentence and blameless in thy judgment" (51:4). Because the psalmist at 94:2 is fully cognizant of the sin of the proud or wicked, he can rightly say, "Rise up, O Judge of the earth; render to the proud their deserts!" (see also 75:7–8).

Since God is a righteous judge (7:11), he will judge righteously (9:4) or uprightly (75:2; see also 58:1). He will judge in righteousness (9:8; 35:24; 96:13; 98:9), with equity (98:9), and in truth (96:13). Therefore, when God gives judgment (82:1), the court proceedings from beginning to end will have been without compromise, partiality, or injustice (67:4; see also 37:32–33).

A second verb "to judge" (GK 1906) occurs eight times. Again, the LORD judges with justice or equity (9:8; 96:10), with care shown for calling forth witnesses to establish the facts in the case (50:4). God's righteousness becomes the standard by which the Israelite king is to judge (72:2). The LORD vindicates his people (54:1; 135:14) and judges the peoples (7:8; see also 110:6).

The verb "examine, try" (GK 1043) occurs nine times. Because the LORD is righteous, he can scrutinize the thoughts and emotions of all (7:9). Because the LORD reigns from heaven, his purview is unlimited. Nothing escapes his gaze. He observes human affairs and assesses them, distinguishing the good from the bad (11:4–5). "On the wicked he will rain coals of fire and brimstone" (11:6), whereas the righteous "shall behold his face" (11:7). The righteous have nothing to fear when the LORD probes or examines them (17:3); they have resolved not to sin and walk continually in the truth (26:2–3).

God may test his people to bring about their purification, just as heat purifies precious metal. "For thou, O God, hast tested us; thou hast tried us as silver is tried" (66:10). The refining fires of life are then listed in a series of metaphors: "Thou didst bring us into the net; thou didst lay afflictions on our loins; thou didst let men ride over our heads; we went through fire and through water" (66:11–12). The refining process is always promising—it guarantees the purity of the metal or of the believer. Here, the believers are brought "to a spacious place" or a place of abundance (66:12). The psalmist has used images from the Exodus and the Conquest to illustrate the refining fires of God (see 81:7; 95:9). The believer may ask the LORD to test him or her to reveal any dross ("offensive way"), and when the believer has passed through the fiery test, the LORD will "lead in the way everlasting" (139:23–24).

The adjective "straight, right" (GK 3838) occurs twenty-five times. Two times the Psalms proclaim that the LORD is "upright" (25:8; 92:15), which must mean that he does not deviate from who he is; he is immutable and trustworthy. Four times his Word is declared to be "upright" (19:8; 33:4; 111:8; 119:137), which must mean that his Word is both true and trustworthy.

In Psalm 25 David pleads that the LORD would not remember his rebellious ways (25:7). David's confident prayer is based in the nature of God as "good and upright" (25:8). "If God was upright," writes Peter C. Craigie, "he could hardly overlook the psalmist's transgressions or the sins of youth; if he was good, he would desire to overlook them as the psalmist bowed in repentance. But God was both good and upright; because he was upright, God could not ignore sin, but because he was good, he could forgive sin."[4]

---

4. Craigie, *Psalms 1–50*, 270.

A related noun "evenness, uprightness, equity" (GK 4797) occurs seven times. According to Psalm 9:7, the LORD has established his throne for the purpose of judgment. That same verse also says that the LORD sits (the NIV renders this verb "reigns") there forever. This suggests that God will always mete out judgment upon the wicked and vindicate the righteous (17:2). We can be confident that the LORD will judge with justice or equity (9:8; 96:10; 98:9; 99:4). In fact, the LORD says so: "I will judge with equity" (75:2).

A related noun (GK 4793) is twice translated "level ground" (26:12; 143:10), once "straight" (27:11), and twice "justice/justly" (45:7; 67:4).

NEW TESTAMENT PARALLEL

The Greek term πιστός (pistos; GK 4412) may be translated "faithful." In the New Testament, because God is faithful (1 Cor 1:9), he will keep believers strong to the end, so that we will be "guiltless in the day of our Lord Jesus Christ" (1:8; see also 1 Thess 5:24). Because God is faithful (1 Cor 10:13), he will provide for us a way out of temptation (10:13). Because God is faithful (2 Cor 1:18), he made real in Christ all the promises he had spoken (Heb 10:23; 11:11). Because the Lord is faithful (2 Thess 3:3), he strengthens and protects believers from the evil one. Because God is faithful (2 Tim 2:13), he will always be true to his character. Because God is the faithful Creator (1 Pet 4:19), believers can commit themselves to him. Because God is faithful (1 John 1:9), he will forgive confessed sin.

As a faithful high priest (Heb 2:17; 3:2), Jesus made atonement for the sins of his people. Jesus is a faithful witness (Rev 1:5; 3:14) to the gospel of God. Jesus is called "Faithful and True" (Rev 19:11).

In 1 Timothy, 2 Timothy, and Titus, Paul writes a number of "trustworthy sayings." "The saying is sure and worthy of full acceptance, that Christ Jesus came into the world to save sinners" (1 Tim 1:15). "The saying is sure and worthy of full acceptance. For to this end we toil and strive, because we have our hope set on the living God, who is the Savior of all men, especially of those who believe" (1 Tim 4:9–10; see also 3:1). "The saying is sure: If we have died with him, we shall also live with him; if we endure, we shall also reign with him" (2 Tim 2:11–12a). "The saying is sure. I desire you to insist on these things, so that those who have believed in God may be careful to apply themselves to good deeds" (Titus 3:8; see also 1:9; Rev 21:5; 22:6).

"If you busy yourself in Psalms, you emerge knowing God." How does one busy oneself in a psalm or in a characteristic of God? You study, you meditate, you sing, and you pray.

MEDITATION

- Is the Lord refining you now? Why? What do you think the outcome will be? How painful has the fire been?
- Do Craigie's words help in making sense of God's justice and grace?
- Which one of the "trustworthy sayings" finds a home in your heart today?

MUSICAL REFLECTION

In 1746 Charles Wesley (1707–1788), prolific British hymn writer, wrote "Rejoice the Lord is King." In light of this chapter, notice the following key words in Wesley's hymn: "truth" in stanza two and "Judge" in the concluding stanza.

> Rejoice, the Lord is King! Your Lord and King adore;
> Rejoice, give thanks and sing, and triumph evermore;
> Lift up your heart, lift up your voice;
> Rejoice, again I say, rejoice!

> Jesus, the Savior, reigns, the God of truth and love;
> When He had purged our stains He took His seat above;
> Lift up your heart, lift up your voice;
> Rejoice, again I say, rejoice!

> His kingdom cannot fail, He rules o'er earth and heaven,
> The keys of death and hell are to our Jesus given;
> Lift up your heart, lift up your voice;
> Rejoice, again I say, rejoice!

> He sits at God's right hand till all His foes submit,
> And bow to His command, and fall beneath His feet:
> Lift up your heart, lift up your voice;
> Rejoice, again I say, rejoice!

> Rejoice in glorious hope! The Lord and Judge shall come,
> And take His servants up to their eternal home.
> Lift up your heart, lift up your voice,
> Rejoice, again I say, rejoice!

PRAYER

Rise up, O righteous Judge, and deliver those falsely accused. Bring to light the truth by exposing the deception of your enemies. Vindicate those who have wrongly suffered for your name. Rescue the oppressed.

I praise you for being true to your character. You are reliable. You do not change. You are faithful and truthful forever.

I am saddened by my sin against your holy name. You are proved right whenever you have judged my sin. I am humbled that you have forgiven my sin and continue to do so. Your goodness compels you to forgive me. Guide me in your truth and teach me your ways.

Rise up, O Judge of the earth, and defend your people. Rise up and help us. Set right all that is wrong. Free all who are shackled by sin and oppression. May the whole earth be filled with your glory! Amen.

∽

What are your song and your prayer?

10

God Is Shepherd

"The LORD is my shepherd" (Psalm 23:1)

THE TERM "SHEPHERD" (GK 8286) is used three times of the LORD in the Psalter (23:1; 28:9; 80:1). Psalm 23:1 ("The LORD is my shepherd") has made this metaphor well known. Ancient Near Eastern kings understood their role to be shepherd of the people, providing for and protecting them. Not surprisingly then, the true King, our LORD, is described as Shepherd (80:1). Psalm 23, a Davidic psalm, also resonates with David's experience as shepherd (see also 1 Sam 16:11, 19; 17:15, 20, 34–37; 2 Sam 7:7–8; Ps 78:70–72).

A shepherd provides for his flock. The second verse affirms that the flock of the LORD will never lack for what they need. For sheep this means water for drinking and green pastures for grazing. "He makes me lie down in green pastures. He leads me beside still waters."

The shepherd also protects his flock. This emphasis is clear in Psalm 78:51–53, a reminiscence of Israel's departure from Egypt. "He smote all the first-born in Egypt, the first issue of their strength in the tents of Ham. Then he led forth his people like sheep, and guided them in the wilderness like a flock. He led them in safety, so that they were not afraid; but the sea overwhelmed their enemies" (see also 77:20; 95:7). Psalm 23:4 mentions the shepherd's rod, an implement to fend off an enemy or attacking beast. The shepherd uses the staff to guide and control his flock.

Psalm 37:3 ties together the themes of provision and protection: "Trust in the LORD, and do good; so you will dwell in the land, and enjoy security" or "safe pasture" (NIV).

Elsewhere, the strength and endurance of the Shepherd are conveyed through the image of Shepherd carrying his flock forever (28:9).

The LORD possesses strength (59:16; 68:34; GK 6437), but more importantly, the LORD is strength. The psalmist proclaims that "the LORD is my strength" (28:7; 59:9, 17; 118:14). The psalmists can proclaim the same truth for the nation/people of Israel (28:8; 46:1; 81:1). In Psalm 21:1 the LORD's strength is synonymous with Israel's victory on the battlefield. The LORD bestows his strength onto his people (29:11).

Those who know the name or character of the LORD trust him (9:10; GK 1053). He is trustworthy because His reliability is unimpeachable. "Thou, O LORD, hast not forsaken those who seek thee." Other psalms offer additional reasons to trust the LORD. "I have trusted in thy steadfast love" (13:5; 21:7; 32:10; 52:8; 143:8). "The LORD is my strength and my shield; in him my heart trusts; so I am helped" (28:7; 115: 9, 10, 11). "We trust in his holy name" (33:21). The LORD is "my refuge and my fortress; my God, in whom I trust" (91:2). "I trust in thy word" (119:42).

Since blessing comes to the one who trusts the LORD (40:4; 84:13), the psalmists charge others to trust Him, by using the imperative form of the verb, the command form (4:5; 37:3, 5; 62:8; 115:9, 10, 11).

Trust in the LORD surpasses trust in man or even princes (44:6; 118:8, 9; 146:3). They are mortal and cannot save, while God is eternal and our Savior.

Book 1 Pss 1–41	Book 2 Pss 42–72	Book 3 Pss 73–89	Book 4 Pss 90–106	Book 5 Pss 107–50
4:5; 9:10; 13:5; 21:7; 22:4, 5, 9; 25:2; 26:2; 27:3; 28:7; 31:6, 14; 32:10; 33:21; 37:3, 5; 40:4; 41:9	44:6; 49:6; 52:7, 8; 55:23; 56:3, 4, 11; 62:8, 10	78:22; 84:13; 86:2	91:2	112:7; 115:8, 9, 10, 11; 118:8, 9; 119:42; 125:1; 135:18; 143:8; 146:3

A shepherd protects his sheep. The noun "sheep" or "flock" (GK 7366) occurs sixteen times in the Psalter. Israel, the people of God, is portrayed as the sheep of God's pasture (74:1; 79:13; 100:3), the "sheep of his hand" (95:7). "Know that the LORD is God! It is he that made us, and we are his; we are his people, and the sheep of his pasture" (100:3). A second noun for "flock" occurs only at 78:52.

Since sheep are vulnerable to attack (44:11, 22; 49:14), they need to be brought out and led to safety (77:20; 78:52; 80:1). The flock has no need to fear evil (23:4), for the LORD, the good shepherd, is with them.

For the Israelite a flock of sheep symbolizes a blessed life (Deut 28:4). This portrait of prosperity is seen at 65:13: "The meadows clothe themselves with flocks, the valleys deck themselves with grain, they shout and sing together for joy." It is seen again at 144:13: "May our garners [barns] be full, providing all manner of store; may our sheep bring forth thousands, and ten thousands in our fields" (see also 107:41).

A shepherd grazes his flock in a pasture (GK 5338). This noun occurs only four times in the Psalms (74:1; 79:13; 95:7; 100:3).

Just by attending church, most Christians have learned a few Hebrew words (without possibly knowing that the words are Hebrew!). *Hallelujah* ("Praise the LORD") and *Immanuel* ("God with us") come to mind. The "with us" portion of "God with us" is transliterated from Hebrew into English as *immanu*. "With us" occurs four times in the Psalter. Psalm 46:7 and 11 read: "The LORD of hosts is with us; the God of Jacob is our fortress." This message is reassuring whenever the natural world (46:2–3) or the nations of the world (46:6) are in upheaval and chaos.

When the LORD allowed his people to return home from a prolonged period of exile, it was said among the nations, "The LORD has done great things for them" (126:2). The Israelites themselves said, "The LORD has done great things for us" (126:3). "For us" here is literally "with us." Exile was a direct result of ingrained and habituated sin. The LORD allowed Israel to be exiled because of his displeasure with her sin. Psalm 85:4 reads: "Restore us again, O God of our salvation, and put away thy indignation toward us." "Toward us" here is literally "with us."

Because the LORD is "with us," as a shepherd is with his sheep, each individual may say, "The LORD is with me." For example, Psalm 42:8 reads, "By day the LORD commands his steadfast love; and at night his song is *with me*—a prayer to the God of my life." Whenever that individual addresses the LORD, he becomes "you" (or "thee"). For example, 73:23 reads, "Yet I am always *with you*; you hold me by my right hand" (NIV; see also 39:12). "There is forgiveness *with thee*" (130:4; see also 130:7). "When I awake, I am still *with thee*" (139:18).

Because the LORD is with us, he may speak of being with each Israelite, with "him" or "her." "My steadfast love shall be *with him*" (89:24). "I will not remove *from him* my steadfast love" (89:33; literally "from with him"). "When he calls to me, I will answer him; I will be *with him* in trouble" (91:15).

The adjective "close, near" occurs nine times (GK 7940). Twice it conveys the sense of "fellowman, neighbor" (15:3; 38:11). Trouble may be near (22:11), but more importantly, the LORD is near to all who call on him (119:151; 145:18). His name is near (75:1), as is his salvation (85:9). The LORD is close to the brokenhearted (34:18). The LORD is close to his people because his people are close to his heart (148:14).

The verb "lead, guide" (GK 5697) occurs eighteen times. The LORD led his people like a flock through the sea (77:20) and out of Egyptian control. "He led them in safety, so that they were not afraid; but the sea overwhelmed their enemies" (78:53). He then guided his people through the wilderness "in the daytime with a cloud" (78:14; see also 78:72; 107:30).

That is a brief resume of the past. What about the present? Because of opposition from enemies David's path has become twisted and unsure. He must rely on God's guidance. "Lead me, O LORD, in thy righteousness because of my enemies; make thy way straight before me" (5:8; see also 23:3). "Lead me on a level path because of my enemies" (27:11).

David must rely on the LORD for safety and protection from his enemies. "Yea, thou art my rock and my fortress; for thy name's sake lead me and guide me" (31:3). "Lead thou me to the rock that is higher than I" (61:2).

God guides through his good Spirit (139:10; 143:10), through light and truth (43:3), and with his counsel (73:24).

He leads now and forever (139:24). His lead is not bound by boundaries. He guides the nations of the earth (67:4).

Another verb meaning "lead, guide" (GK 5633) occurs only twice (23:2; 31:3). Both verbs occur together in 31:3.

Isaiah 53:6 reminds us that sheep go astray. If we follow the metaphor, we are mindful of our moral failures—we are sinners who have strayed from God. But God, the Good Shepherd, protects us by forgiving that sin. The Psalter uses ten different words to describe his forgiveness of my sin.

The verb "blot out" (GK 4681), which appears six times, is used in two ways in the Psalms: (1) to obliterate from memory (9:5; 69:28; 109:13); (2) transgressions no more remembered by God against the sinner (51:1, 9; 109:14).

The verb "cover over, to make atonement" (GK 4105) occurs only three times (65:3; 78:38; 79:9). The one whose sins are forgiven is chosen to come near to God and enjoy the blessings of his presence (65:4). This is true reconciliation. In the Old Testament system of sacrifices, the removal of sin was a visual object lesson. Because the wages of sin is death (Rom 6:23), I must die for my sin. But God is gracious. He accepts the death of an animal as a ransom for my life. The life of a sacrificial animal was required in exchange for the life of the worshipper. This is atonement.

The verb "lift, carry, take" (GK 5951) is used forty-nine times in the Psalter, but only five times with the sense of take or take away iniquity, that is, to forgive (25:18; 32:1, 5; 85:2; 99:8). God lifts up and carries away our sin and its associated guilt and shame. That is quite a picture! If the sin is carried or taken away, then it is no longer present in my life or unresolved. It is gone.

The verb "to cover" (Gk 4059) occurs seventeen times in the Psalms, but only two times with the sense of covering (concealing) sin, that is, to forgive sin (32:1 [see also v. 5]; 85:2). It is never good for men to conceal their sin (32:5). In fact, "he who conceals his transgressions will not prosper" (Prov 28:13a). Rather, we are admonished to confess our sin and renounce it (Prov 28:13b). On the other hand, it is good for us whenever God conceals or covers our sin (Prov 17:9). Nehemiah prays that God would "not cover up the guilt" of the nation's enemies or "blot out their sin" (Neh 4:5).

The verb "forgive, pardon" occurs only twice (25:11; 103:3), with an adjective, "forgiving" (86:5), and a noun, "forgiveness" (130:4), rounding out the list (GK 6142, 6143, 6145). The adjective is an interesting word. It is a word which exhibits the "professional pattern." Allow me to explain. If I take the verb "to judge," and then apply this pattern to it, I have the noun "judge," someone who is a professional at judging. If we apply this concept to the verb "to forgive," God is a professional at forgiving. "For thou, O LORD, art good and forgiving, abounding in steadfast love to all who call on thee" (86:5).

The verb "be, or become, far, distant" is used once with respect to sin. "As far as the east is from the west, so far does he remove our transgressions from us" (103:12). (The psalmists do not want the LORD to be far from them: 22:11, 19; 35:22; 38:21; 71:12.)

The verbs "wash" (GK 3891) and "cleanse" (GK 3197) are paired in 51:2, 7, and do not appear elsewhere in the Psalter.

The verb "to think, account" (GK 3108) occurs eighteen times, but only twice with the sense "to count." "Blessed is the man to whom the LORD imputes [counts] no iniquity" (32:2). "I am reckoned [counted] among those who go down to the Pit" (88:4). Closely tied to this verb is the verb "to remember" (GK 2349), which is used once with the sense of forgiveness. "Remember not the sins of my youth or my transgressions" (25:7).

The good news is that God forgives. The bad news is that I have sinned. Since sin is a complex, multi-dimensional reality, the Psalter uses multiple words to describe our sin.

The noun "iniquity" (GK 6411) occurs thirty-one times. This is a noun which suggests distortion or perversion. The noun "wickedness" (GK 224) occurs twenty-eight times. The noun "transgression" (GK 7322) occurs fourteen times in the Psalter. This is a noun which suggests rebellion against God. The noun "sin" (GK 2633) occurs thirteen times. This is a noun which suggests turning away from the true path. The adjective "insolent, presumptuous" (GK 2294) is used seven times in the Psalms for the arrogant (86:14; 119:21, 51, 69, 78, 85, 122), and once for willful, arrogant sin (19:13).

NEW TESTAMENT PARALLEL

The word "shepherd" (GK 4478) occurs eighteen times. Shepherds beheld the Christ child, the babe of Bethlehem, and then bore witness to him (Luke 2:8, 15, 18, 20).

Jesus had compassion on the crowds that followed him, because they were harassed and helpless, "like sheep without a shepherd" (Matt 9:36; Mark 6:34). Jesus predicted his death and Peter's denial by quoting Zechariah 13:7: "I will strike the shepherd, and the sheep of the flock will be scattered" (Matt 26:31; Mark 14:27). At his second coming, like a shepherd Jesus will separate the sheep from the goats (Matt 25:32).

Jesus declared, "I am the good shepherd" (John 10:11, 14). The book of Hebrews calls Jesus the "great Shepherd of the sheep" (13:20). Peter refers to Jesus as the "Shepherd and Overseer" of our souls (1 Pet 2:25). As a true shepherd (John 10:2) Jesus was willing to lay down his life for the safety of the flock (10:11 [contrast this with v. 12], 15). The flock of Jesus knows him and listens to his voice (10:16).

Pastors are shepherds (Eph 4:11). They are responsible for the care and feeding of the flock.

The noun "sheep" (GK 4585) occurs thirty-nine times (fifteen in John 10 alone). Sheep are presented as helpless (Matt 9:36), lost (Matt 10:6; 15:24), having gone astray (1 Pet 2:25), scattered (Matt 26:31), vulnerable (Matt 10:16; John 10:12), objects for sale (Rev 18:13) or slaughter (Acts 8:32; Rom 8:36), and yet loved by our Lord, Jesus Christ, the great Shepherd of the sheep!

The Lamb of God offered himself for slaughter so that wayward sheep might join the flock of the Great Shepherd!

∽

"If you busy yourself in Psalms, you emerge knowing God." How does one busy oneself in a psalm or in a characteristic of God? You study, you meditate, you sing, and you pray.

MEDITATION

- Why do you trust God?
- How is your sense of direction? Think of a time when you ran your life off the road. How did God pull you out of the ditch?
- In what ways has God guided you?
- Which one of the ten images of forgiveness gives you the greatest sense of relief? Do you have an image you could add to this list? Read Micah 7:19.
- What type of sheep have you been?

MUSICAL REFLECTION

In 1836 Dorothy Thrupp (1779–1847), who lived in London, England, wrote the hymn, "Savior, Like a Shepherd Lead Us."

> Savior, like a shepherd lead us; much we need Thy tender care;
> in Thy pleasant pastures feed us; for our use Thy folds prepare:

Blessed Jesus, blessed Jesus, Thou has bought us, Thine we are; blessed Jesus, blessed Jesus, Thou hast bought us, Thine we are.

We are Thine—do Thou befriend us; be the Guardian of our way; keep Thy flock, from sin defend us; seek us when we go astray: Blessed Jesus, blessed Jesus, hear, O hear us when we pray; blessed Jesus, blessed Jesus, hear, O hear us when we pray.

Thou has promised to receive us, poor and sinful tho we be; Thou hast mercy to relieve us, grace to cleanse and pow'r to free: Blessed Jesus, blessed Jesus, early let us turn to Thee; blessed Jesus, blessed Jesus, early let us turn to Thee.

Early let us seek Thy favor; early let us do Thy will; blessed Lord and only Savior, with Thy love our bosoms fill: Blessed Jesus, blessed Jesus, Thou hast loved us; love us still; blessed Jesus, blessed Jesus, Thou hast loved us, love us still.

PRAYER

"The Lord is my shepherd, I shall not want." God, I remember saying to my Mom, as she was teaching me this psalm, "That is not very nice, not to want God." I do want you. I long for you. It is so refreshing, rejuvenating, and revitalizing to read again how *you* want to be with us, even in our troubles. We have so much trouble; there is so much evil around us. Yet, we do not have to fear evil, for you are with us. God you will lead us out of trouble to green pastures and to still waters. You will lead us closer to your side, deep into your presence.

In your presence I recognize my sinfulness. Yet, you are gracious to forgive. I am amazed that you use so many words to convey to us the totality of your forgiveness. I so love that when you blot out my sin, you obliterate from memory my transgression.

Sin means death. I should die for my sin, and yet you took my death upon yourself. You died for me. When you lift up and take away my sin and its shame and guilt, I am free to live unencumbered.

My Lord and my God, who is like you? You are God, and there is no other. You are majestic in holiness. You are awesome in glory. And the greatest wonder of all wonders is that you want to be with us. In fact, it brings you pleasure! I humble myself before you my God and my King Shepherd.

∼

What are your song and your prayer?

11

God Is Present

> "The eyes of the LORD are toward the righteous,
> and his ears are toward their cry" (Psalm 34:15)

GOD IS SPIRIT (DEUT 4:15–16; John 4:24; 1 Tim 1:17; 6:16); he is without body. This chapter will focus, however, on how the Psalter speaks anthropomorphically of the eyes, ears, nose, mouth, hands, arm, feet, heart, and face of the LORD.

EYES

Unlike the idols, which have eyes (GK 6524) but cannot see (115:5; 135:16), the LORD does see. His eyes examine both the wicked and the righteous (11:4; 66:7), who yearn for vindication, knowing that the LORD's eyes "see the right" (17:2). "The eyes of the LORD are toward the righteous" (34:15); "the eye of the LORD is on those who fear him" (33:18). The weak and needy are precious in his sight (72:13–14), as is "the death of his saints" (116:15). He sees the unformed body in the mother's womb (139:16).

The one who sees formed the eye for sight (94:9). Every living creature looks to the LORD for food at the proper time (145:15). David promised to keep his eyes "on the faithful in the land" (101:6). The psalmist prays for illumination that he may see wonderful things in the law (119:18). He asks the LORD to turn his "eyes from looking at vanities" (119:37). David's eyes are fixed on the Sovereign LORD (141:8).

The common verb "see" (GK 8011) appears one hundred times in the Psalms. Twenty-two times the LORD is subject of the verb. The LORD has seen (31:7), does see (10:14), and can be commanded (Please!) to see (9:13; 25:18, 19; 59:3; 80:14; 84:9; 119:153, 159; 139:24; 142:4). He sees the psalmists' enemies (9:13; 25:19; 35:17, 22; 59:3), their trouble and grief (10:14), their affliction and distress (25:18; 106:44), their suffering (119:153), and their obedience (119:159; 139:24).

The verb "look down" appears four times in the Psalter. The LORD looks down from heaven (14:2; 53:2) to see if any seek him. He looked down from his sanctuary on high, that is heaven, "to hear the groans of the prisoners, to set free those who were doomed to die" (102:20). Righteousness looks down from heaven (85:11).

EARS

The idols of the nations have ears, but cannot hear (115:6; 135:17). The one who implanted the ear, however, does hear (94:9). His ears are attentive to the cry of the righteous (34:15). This noun (GK 265) appears twenty-two times in the Psalms.

In Psalms three different verbs combine with the noun "ear" to convey the sense of hearing. (1) "come" (18:6; GK 995); (2) "incline, bend" (17:6; 31:2; 71:2; 86:1; 88:2; 102:2; 116:2; GK 5742); (3) "incline, attend" (10:17; 130:2; GK 7992). Indeed, the LORD does hear!

The common verb "hear" (GK 9048) occurs seventy-nine times. Thirty-nine times God is the subject of the verb. Fifteen times an imperative is used: "Hear, O LORD!" (30:10). He is "commanded" to hear "my prayer" (4:1; 39:12; 54:2; 84:8; 102:1; 143:1); "my voice" (27:7; 119:149; 130:2); "my cry" (28:2; 61:1); "my plea" (17:1); "my word" (17:6; the NIV renders this word "prayer"); and once "me" (64:1). Twice the LORD uses the imperative upon his people (50:7; 81:8).

NOSE

The idols of the nations have noses, but they cannot smell (115:6). In short they are listless, lifeless blocks of wood. The LORD has a nose. In Hebrew thinking, the nose is the seat of anger. This explains why the noun "nose" (GK 678), which occurs thirty-five times in Psalms, can be translated as "anger" twenty-four times (all but four referencing divine anger) and "wrath" four times (all divine). For example, Psalm 76:7 reads: "But thou, terrible art thou! Who can stand before thee when once thy anger is roused?"

Twice in Psalm 18, both in the context of earth-convulsing, rock-shattering theophany, the nostrils of the LORD are mentioned. "Smoke went up from his nostrils" (18:8). "Then the channels of the sea were seen, and the foundations of the world were laid bare, at thy rebuke, O LORD, at the blast of the breath of thy nostrils" (18:15).

Three times in the psalms the LORD is described as "slow to anger" (86:15; 103:8; 145:8). The Hebrew literally says of the LORD that he is "long of nose/nostrils." If we think of the nose as the seat of anger, as the Hebrews did, then a long nose would require a prolonged period of time for the blood to rush to the nose, the color of rage (red), or for the momentum of rage to cause the flaring of nostrils. "Slow to anger" becomes an acceptable translation, even if it is a bit colorless! (The NIV translation of Psalm 10:4 is also a bit bland. "In his pride" is literally, "in the height of his nose." The English idiom "his nose is stuck in the air" is dynamically equivalent.)

The creed of Psalm 86:15; 103:8; and 145:8 is heard also at Exodus 34:6, Numbers 14:18, Nehemiah 9:17, Jonah 4:2, and Joel 2:13. Reader, please take the time to read these verses!

With a nose, one usually possesses the sense of smell. The verb "to smell" occurs only at 115:6.

The Hebrews also perceived the kidneys [GK 4000] as a seat of emotion and affection. The noun "kidneys" appears five times in the Psalter, though never of God, and never translated as such by the NIV (7:9 ["minds"]; 16:7 ["heart"]; 26:2 ["heart"]; 73:21 ["spirit"]; 139:13 ["inmost being"]).

MOUTH

The idols have mouths, but cannot speak (115:5; 135:16–17). They are mute, without life to even exhale a word. The LORD has a mouth, however, and speaks! (The noun "mouth" [GK 7023] occurs sixty-seven times, but only seven of these refer to the mouth of the LORD.) He spoke the cosmos into existence. "By the word of the LORD the heavens were made, and all their host by the breath of his mouth" (33:6). With "devouring fire from his mouth" (18:8), he authors judgment upon the forces of evil.

His words are obvious proof of his mouth (105:5; 138:4)! More than any other psalm, Psalm 119 celebrates the words of the LORD: law, testimonies, precepts, statutes, commandments, ordinances, words, and promises. "With my lips I declare all the ordinances of thy mouth" (119:13). "The law of thy mouth is better to me than thousands of gold and silver pieces" (119:72). "In thy steadfast love spare my life, that I may keep the testimonies of thy mouth" (119:88). The verb "to taste" appears but once (34:8).

The idols cannot utter a sound with their throats (115:7). This noun "throats" appears only three other times in the Psalms. The throat of David's enemies is an open grave (5:9), "for there is no truth in their mouth." On the other hand, David's throat is parched calling out to the LORD for help (69:3). The praise of God is in the throats of his saints (149:6).

The verb "answer" (GK 6699) appears thirty-six times in the Psalter (only once is the answerer human—119:42). With but just two exceptions (18:41; 22:2), the LORD has answered (118:21), does answer (20:6), will answer (86:7), or is called upon to answer (4:1; 13:3; 27:7; 55:2; 60:5; 69:13, 16, 17; 86:1; 102:2; 108:6; 119:148; 143:1, 7). At 69:17; 102:2; and 143:7 the LORD is called upon to answer, and to answer quickly (this word quickly also appears at 79:8 and 106:13).

The verb "be silent" (GK 3087) occurs eight times. When the psalmists cry out to the LORD, he hears and answers. But what if he does not respond? Is the silence a sign of his displeasure? Has he abandoned his covenant people?

When the enemy rises up, the psalmist may request divine intervention by saying, "Be not deaf to me" (28:1; 39:12) or "Be not silent" (35:22; 83:1). "Be not silent, O God of my praise! For wicked and deceitful mouths are opened against me; speaking against me with lying tongues. They beset me with words of hate, and attack me without cause" (109:1–3).

In Psalm 50:4 God summons both heavens and earth as witnesses in the case against his people. The Divine Judge (50:6) will also offer his own testimony, "Hear, O my people, and I will speak, O Israel, I will testify against you" (50:7).

God will no longer remain silent (50:3). He will speak his case! If Israel thought his silence was proof that he was unconcerned about sin or they had avoided his notice (50:21a), they are wrong on both accounts. His silence was a mere delay in judgment. "But now I rebuke you, and lay the charge before you" (50:21c).

Psalm 135:17 declares that the idols have no breath in their mouths. The word for breath here is the same word for God's spirit in 51:11 and for winds in 148:8 (GK 8120). The idols are lifeless—they do not possess an animating spirit. In contrast, God is spirit. He is alive. He is also the creator of reality (33:6), which includes the swirling winds and the spirits which animate every human life!

God formed the cosmos "by the breath of his mouth" (33:6). His presence or Spirit is pervasive (139:7) throughout that creation. "When thou sendest forth thy Spirit, they are created; and thou renewest the face of the ground" (104:30). So He gives and renews life, but he also takes it away. "When thou takest away their breath, they die and return to their dust" (104:29). "At the blast of the breath of thy nostrils," he rebukes his enemies (18:15). He also directs human life. God's "good spirit" leads his people "on a level path" (143:10).

HANDS

The idols of the nations have hands, but are powerless (115:7). They are mere products of the hands of men (115:4; 135:15). The LORD, on the other hand, exercises power, ultimate power. He has hands (GK 3338).

The creation of the world is evidence of the LORD's power. "Of old thou didst lay the foundation of the earth, and the heavens are the work of thy hands" (102:25; see also 19:1). "In his hand are the depths of the earth; the heights of the mountains are his also. The sea is his, for he made it; for his hands formed the dry land" (95:4–5; see also 104:24). The Psalms also bear witness to the creation of mankind. "Thy hands have made and fashioned me" (119:73; see also 8:4–8).

The LORD providentially sustains the world he created. The vast array of the earth's creatures look to the LORD "to give them their food in due season" (104:27). "When thou givest to them, they gather it up; when thou openest thy hand, they are filled with good things" (104:28; 145:15–16).

The LORD is purposefully active in the world, engaged in work, the nature of which the psalmists do not always specify. For example, Psalm 143:5: "I remember the days of old, I meditate on all that thou hast done; I muse on what thy hands have wrought." Psalm 92:4 is the same. "For thou, O LORD, hast made me glad by thy work; at the works of thy hands I sing for joy" (see also 28:5; 111:7; 138:8).

God promised Abraham that his descendants would be His special people and they would one day live in a delightful and beautiful land. The LORD fought against the Canaanites to secure the land, to make real the promise to Abraham. "Thou with thy own hand didst drive out the nations, but them thou didst plant; thou didst afflict the peoples, but them thou didst set free" (44:2).

Throughout Israel's history the LORD continued to fight for his people in their struggle to survive. Israel's past victories, or should I say God's successes, prompted the psalmists to trust the LORD during their present struggles. "Stretch forth thy hand from on high, rescue me and deliver me from the many waters, from the hand of aliens" (144:7; see also 10:12, 14; 17:14; 109:27). "Though I walk in the midst of trouble, thou dost preserve my life; thou dost stretch out thy hand against the wrath of my enemies, and thy right hand delivers me" (138:7). "My times are in thy hand; deliver me from the hand of my enemies and persecutors!" (31:15).

The LORD's hand, his mighty hand (136:12; 78:42; 89:13), cares for (95:7; 88:5), disciplines (32:4; 38:2; 39:10; 106:26), guides (139:10), helps (119:173), redeems (31:5), restores (80:17), sustains (89:21), and upholds (37:24) his chosen ones. At the same time, his mighty hand may strike down his foes (74:11; 75:8). The term "hand/hands" occurs ninety-four times; "fingers" only twice (8:3; 144:1).

RIGHT HAND

The term "right hand" figures prominently in the Psalms, appearing forty-two times (GK 3545). With his right hand, the LORD bestows benefits and blessings (16:11; 89:25), fights victoriously (44:3; 74:11; 91:7), guides (78:54), holds (139:10), plants (80:15), saves (17:7; 20:6; 60:5; 108:6; 138:7), secures (16:8; 80:17), seizes foes (21:8), sustains (18:35), upholds (63:8), and works mighty deeds (77:10; 98:1; 118:15, 16). The right hand of the LORD is exalted (89:13) and filled with righteousness (48:10).

ARM

Closely related to the hand is, of course, the arm (GK 2432). The noun occurs fourteen times. The noun suggests power or strength, whether human (18:34; 37:17; 10:15; 83:8) or divine (71:18; 79:11; 89:13). Notice the contrast between human power and the sufficiency of divine power at 44:3: "For not by their own sword did they win the land, nor did their own arm give them victory; but thy right hand, and thy arm, and the light of thy countenance; for thou didst delight in them."

The LORD's arm is holy (98:1). It is set apart, therefore, for works of salvation (98:1), redemption (77:15; 89:10; 136:12), and strengthening his anointed one (89:21).

FEET

The nations' idols have feet, but remain motionless, inert. The noun "feet" (GK 8079) occurs thirty-one times in the Psalter, but only three relate to the LORD's feet. Using language that evokes fear and awe, Psalm 18 describes the LORD's coming to the Red Sea and to Mount Sinai to judge the powers of evil and to deliver his people to himself for a holy relationship. "He bowed the heavens, and came down; thick darkness was under his feet" (v. 9).

God may go before his people without leaving a trace of his presence. "Thy way was through the sea, thy path through the great waters; yet thy footprints were unseen" (77:19). When the mighty waters of the sea close over footprints, the tracks become unknown, invisible. The proof of God's unperceived presence, however, is clear to everyone. His people are safe, and the Egyptians drowned.

According to 2 Chronicles 9:18, Solomon's throne had six steps, and a footstool of gold was attached to it. Psalms 99:5 and 132:7 (see also 110:1) speak of the footstool of the LORD. The ark of the covenant may be understood as a footstool for the enthroned divine king. Psalms 80:1 and 99:1 say that the LORD sits enthroned between the cherubim (which stood atop the ark, with wings outstretched). If we follow the imagery of this analogy, then the ark would be our LORD's footstool. First Chronicles 28:2 supports this view. In this verse David remembers his intentions to build the temple: "I had it in my heart to build a house of rest for the ark of the covenant of the LORD, and for the footstool of our God; and I made preparations for building."

The temple proper could also be envisioned as the LORD's footstool. With respect to the temple, Isaiah writes, "The glory of Lebanon shall come to you, the cypress, the plane, and the pine, to beautify the place of my sanctuary; and I will make the place of my feet glorious" (60:13).

The city of Jerusalem may also be considered as the footstool of the LORD. Lamentations grieves over the destruction of the city of Jerusalem and the deportation of its inhabitants. Listen to 2:1: "How the Lord in his anger has set the daughter of Zion under a cloud! He has cast down from heaven to earth the splendor of Israel; he has not remembered his footstool in the day of his anger." Isaiah 66:1 depicts the whole earth as the footstool (see also Matt 5:35). "Heaven is my throne and the earth is my footstool."

HEART

Two nouns for "heart" are used in the Psalter. The first one (GK 4213) is used 102 times and the second one (GK 4222) thirty-five times. Only the first one is used of the Lord. Psalm 33:11 says, "The counsel of the LORD stands for ever, the thoughts of his heart to all generations." This is the only reference in the Psalms to the heart of the LORD. Interestingly, the same psalm reminds us that the LORD "fashions the hearts of all" (33:15), and in the LORD "our heart is glad" (33:21).

FACE

Since the LORD has eyes, ears, nose, and mouth, he has a face (GK 7156). "The upright shall behold his face" (11:7), that is, they will enjoy the sweet fellowship of his presence (see 17:15). The psalmists desire this blessing for themselves (27:8; 42:2) and for others (24:6; 105:4). "I have sought your face with all of my heart" (119:58, NIV). The righteous seek the LORD's face, but the LORD has set his face against the evil-doer, "to cut off the remembrance of them from the earth" (34:16).

The famous blessing of Numbers 6 reads in part, "The LORD make his face to shine upon you" (6:25a). When this happens, the radiant glory of the LORD's presence is reflected in the face of the worshipper. "Look to him, and be radiant; so your faces shall never be ashamed" (34:5). The experience of Moses is the proof. Whenever he entered into the presence of the LORD to speak with him, and then came out, his face was radiant (Exod. 34:29–35).

The joy that comes from basking in the LORD's grace, favor, and blessing may be seen in the worshipper's smile. This joy is conveyed at 104:15 through the mention of an agricultural triplet: wine, oil, and bread. "Wine to gladden the heart of man, oil to make his face shine, and bread to strengthen man's heart."

The LORD's face shines in the Psalms. For example, 67:1 says, "May God be gracious to us and bless us and make his face shine upon us" (see also 4:6; 31:16; 44:3; 80:3, 7, 19; 89:15; 118:27; and 119:135).

Twice in the Psalms, the gift of divine light is synonymous with life. "Lighten my eyes, lest I sleep the sleep of death" (13:3b). "The commandment of the LORD is pure, enlightening the eyes" (19:8b).

The opposite of "shine" is "hide" (GK 6259). When the LORD "hides" his face (or just hides), it is a sign of rejection and punishment for sin. For example 143:7 says, "Make haste to answer me, O LORD! My spirit fails. Hide not thy face from me, lest I be like those who go down to the Pit" (13:2; 27:9; 30:7; 44:24; 69:17; 88:14; 89:46; 102:2; see also 10:11; 22:24; 104:29).

On occasion the verb "hide" can be used favorably. It speaks of divine protection. David prays that the LORD "hide" him in the shadow of the divine wings (17:8). David is certain that in the day of trouble the LORD will "hide" him in the shelter of his tabernacle (27:5) or in the shelter of his presence (31:20). "Hide me from the secret plots of the wicked, from the scheming of evildoers" (64:2). It is used once to suggest forgiveness. David prays that the LORD not factor certain of his sins into the justice equation. "Hide thy face from my sins, and blot out all my iniquities" (51:9). It is used once for the orienting revelation of God's word in a strange and disorienting world. "I am a sojourner on earth; hide not thy commandments from me!" (119:19).

For Israel's neighbors, the face of a deity meant the face of the image of that god. To seek the face of a deity meant an opportunity to see the face of that sacred image. In Israel this physical aspect was eliminated. The LORD was invisibly present amongst his people. When the Israelite worshipper saw the LORD, then, he or she experienced his presence, his help, and his grace. "The face of God is the revelation of the grace of God."[1]

NEW TESTAMENT PARALLEL

In the New Testament, the word "face" (GK 4725) appears seventy-six times. A small number of these are important to our study in this chapter. During the Transfiguration, Jesus' face shone like the sun (Matt 17:2; Luke 9:29). This transformation was proof that the presence of God had enveloped the mountainside. Paul can say that our knowledge of the glory of God is seen in the face of Christ (2 Cor 4:6).

---

1. Kraus, *Theology of the Psalms*, 39.

God Is Present

Peter, James, and John saw the presence of God reflected in the face of Jesus. Angels always see the face of God in heaven (Matt 18:10), that is, they are constantly aware of His presence.

That "face-to-face" presence we already reflect (2 Cor 3:18), but it is also the glory we await and hope for in eternity (1 Cor 13:12). The wicked, on the other hand, will be forever shut out from the presence of God (2 Thess 1:9), a presence they shunned and feared (Rev 6:16).

In Revelation as John describes eternity, he says, "There shall no more be anything accursed, but the throne of God and of the Lamb shall be in it, and his servants shall worship him; they shall see his face, and his name shall be on their foreheads" (22:3–4).

"If you busy yourself in Psalms, you emerge knowing God." How does one busy oneself in a psalm or in a characteristic of God? You study, you meditate, you sing, and you pray.

MEDITATION

Which one of these parts of the divine body is meaningful for your faith today?

MUSICAL REFLECTION

Carrie E. Breck (1855–1934), mother of five daughters and author of 2,000 poems, composed the words to the hymn "Face to Face."

> Face to face with Christ, my Savior, face to face—what will it be? When with rapture I behold Him, Jesus Christ who died for me!

> Only faintly now I see Him, with the darkling veil between; but a blessed day is coming, when His glory shall be seen.

> What rejoicing in His presence, when are banished grief and pain, when the crooked ways are straightened and the dark things shall be plain.

> Face to face—O blissful moment! Face to face—to see and know; face to face with my Redeemer, Jesus Christ who loves me so.

> Chorus: Face to face I shall behold Him, far beyond the starry sky; face to face, in all His glory, I shall see Him by and by!

PRAYER

My Lord, my God, the more I study your character, the more I am in awe of you. On the clouds in majesty you hold all of creation with just a word, yet you reveal yourself anthropomorphically, so we might better relate to you.

You are omnipresent. You have eyes that see the evil and the righteous, the needy, and the unborn. You show us that you see our trouble and grief, our afflictions and distress, and our obedience.

You are omniscient. You have ears to hear our joy, our sorrows, and our prayers.

You are omnipotent. When you speak, the heavens and the earth do your bidding.

You have a long nose God, and I am so grateful, for you are slow to become angry with your people, especially me!

To gaze upon your face, Lord, to be in your presence, this is the height of human experience. My God, to me you have allowed glimpses of your face. O, that I had the words to describe the joy I felt at every level of my being. I have known the tingling sensation, a warm blanket enveloping me, a heat that penetrates through me. Emotionally I have felt the heights of pure joy. I have felt loved, and I have wanted to share that love with others.

O God, I long for the day when we see you face to face. How could it be that we receive that inheritance! My God, bless your holy name!

∼

What are your song and your prayer?

12

The House of the LORD

"I rejoiced with those who said to me, 'Let us go
to the house of the LORD.'" (Psalm 122:1)

BOTH KINGS AND GODS live in houses. The home of a king is called a palace, while the home of a god is called a temple or a sanctuary. The house of the LORD refers naturally to his temple in Jerusalem. "I love the house where you live, O LORD, the place where your glory dwells" (26:8). Besides being a dwelling place, it was also a house of worship, where God's people gathered to worship him. "But I, by your great mercy, will come into your house, in reverence will I bow down toward your holy temple" (5:7).

The LORD's house in Jerusalem was unique; it was, therefore, holy (93:5). It was to be the only place of national worship and sacrifice acceptable to the LORD. "I will come to *your* temple [house] with burnt offerings and fulfill my vows to you" (66:13).

Three times annually Israelites would journey to Jerusalem, to Zion, and there offer praise to their King and Lord (Exod 23:14–17). The Psalms make mention of these journeys, these pilgrimages. "I rejoiced with those who said to me, 'Let us go to the house of the LORD'" (122:1). "These things I remember as I pour out my soul: how I used to go with the multitude, leading the procession to the house of God, with shouts of joy and thanksgiving among the festive throng" (42:4; see also 55:14).

Once the journey had been made, and the psalmist had climbed the temple mount and stood in the dwelling of the LORD (15:3), then he could savor the sweet fellowship of the LORD. This communion was so real that the psalmists longed to live permanently in the presence of the LORD. "One thing I ask of the LORD, this is what I seek: that I may dwell in the house of the LORD all the days of my life, to gaze upon the beauty of the LORD and to seek him in his temple" (27:4). "Blessed are those who dwell in your house; they are ever praising you" (84:4; see also 65:4; 84:10).

The presence of the LORD is "goodness and mercy" (23:6); it is life and security (what is stronger than a cedar of Lebanon?). "The righteous will flourish like a palm tree, they will grow like a cedar of Lebanon; planted in the house of the LORD, they will flourish in the courts of our God" (92:12–13).

David desires the LORD's presence all the days of his earthly sojourn (23:6). He also desires that same presence beyond the veil of this realm. He confidently asserts that he "will dwell in the house of the LORD forever" (23:6). Now, to what extent David understood life beyond this one, I do not know. The image provoked by these words is, however, encouraging. Who can imagine an eternity more glorious than gazing upon the LORD's beauty forever?

The Hebrew word "house" (GK 1074) is used twenty-two times to refer to the LORD's dwelling in Jerusalem (5:7; 23:6; 26:8; 27:4; 30 [superscription]; 36:8; 42:4; 52:8; 55:14; 65:4; 66:13; 69:9; 84:4, 10; 92:13; 93:5; 116:19; 118:26; 122:1, 9; 134:1; 135:2).

The Hebrew word "palace, temple" (GK 2121) occurs thirteen times in the Psalms. It may be translated "palace," when referring to a king's dwelling, or "temple," when referring to God's dwelling. Three times it is "palace" (45:8, 15; 144:12); ten times "temple" (5:7; 11:4; 18:6; 27:4; 29:9; 48:9; 65:4; 68:29; 79:1; 138:2). This word is derived from the Sumerian language where it meant "great house" or "big house." Who lived in a house bigger or greater than the king or a god?

"I will bow down toward your holy temple and will praise your name for your love and your faithfulness, for you have exalted above all things your name and your word" (138:2).

The noun "dwelling place, tabernacle" (GK 5438) is used once of God's dwelling place in Shiloh (78:60) and seven times of his dwelling in Jerusalem (43:3; 46:4; 84:1; 132:5, 7). The tabernacle/temple is the place where the glory of the LORD dwells (26:8); it is the dwelling place of the Name (74:7).

"Sanctuary" (GK 5219) appears five times (68:35; 73:17; 74:7; 78:69; 96:6). This word conveys the sense of a holy or sacred place.

The most important piece of furniture in the Temple was the ark of the covenant. It was the only piece of furniture in the Holy of Holies, the most holy sanctum of the Temple. The ark was a chest of acacia wood—about 3 ¾ feet long and 2 ½ feet wide and high (Exod 25:10). This chest was covered with pure gold, both inside and out (Exod 25:11). Two golden cherubs (angelic figures) stood above the ark, one at one end and the second at the other (25:19). These angelic figures had their wings spread upward, overshadowing the ark with them (25:20).

The ark and the cherubs (the Hebrew plural is cherubim) together suggest the throne of God. "The LORD reigns, let the nations tremble; he sits enthroned between the cherubim, let the earth shake" (99:1; see also 80:1; 18:10). Psalm 132:8 is the only place in the Psalms where the ark is specifically mentioned.

It is quite possible that when the psalmists refer to finding shelter or refuge beneath the wings of God (17:8; 36:7; 57:1; 61:4; 63:7; 91:4), they have the wings of the cherubs in mind. Psalm 61:4 may add weight to this consideration. "I long to dwell in your tent forever and take refuge in the shelter of your wings." The precursor to the Temple was the tabernacle, a tent which was moved from place to place as Israel wandered in the wilderness. The noun "tent" (GK 185) occurs eighteen times in the Psalter, but only five refer to a place of worship (15:1 ["sanctuary"]; 27:5, 6 ["tabernacle"]; 61:4 ["tent"]; 78:60 ["tent" parallels "tabernacle"]).

The image could be drawn from the bird which spreads its wings over its young (Matt 23:37; Luke 13:34). This possibility takes flight at Psalm 91:4, which reads, "He will cover you with his feathers, and under his wings you will find refuge; his faithfulness will be your shield and rampart."

Whatever the origin of the image, and both could be in play depending on context, the LORD is an asylum, a safe place in the midst of trouble. "Have mercy on me, O God, have mercy on me, for in you my soul takes refuge. I will take refuge in the shadow of your wings until the disaster has passed" (57:1).

The term "shade" (GK 7498) appears ten times in the Psalter. Three times it is metaphoric for the transitoriness of life. "Man is like a breath; his days are like a fleeting shadow" (144:4; see also 102:11; 109:23). Six times it is used for protection the LORD offers. Five times we find protection in the shadow of the LORD's wings (17:8; 36:7; 57:1; 63:7; 91:1). "I will take refuge in the shadow of your wings until the disaster has passed" (57:1b). Once the LORD's help is likened to shade from the sun's rays (121:5). Psalm 80:10 is non-theological.

Psalm 15:1 raises the question, "Who may dwell in your sanctuary?" The balance of the psalm provides the answer. In short, "he who does what is righteous" (15:2). Psalm 5:4 has already pronounced that with the LORD "the wicked cannot dwell." The righteous long "to dwell" in the LORD's tent forever (61:4).

The noun "altar" (GK 4640) is used five times. The tabernacle or the temple had two altars: the altar of incense and the altar of burnt offerings. The altar of incense, being in the holy place, would have been off-limits to all, save the priesthood (see 141:2). At Psalm 26:6 the psalmist circles about the altar for sacrifice, proclaiming aloud his praise of the LORD. The psalmist says, "I love the house where you live, O LORD, the place where your glory dwells" (26:8). In Psalm 43 the poet pictures a trip to the temple, "the place where you dwell" (43:3). There he will approach the altar for sacrifice and praise God to the tune of the harp (43:4). Psalm 118:27 speaks of a festal procession up to the horns of the altar.

At Psalm 51:19, bulls are sacrificed on the altar of burnt offerings. The psalmist envies the birds that have built a nest near the altar (84:3).

The temple also featured a light-source, the ten lampstands (1 Kings 7:49). Even though the Psalms do not explicitly mention the lampstands, the concept of light is an important theme. In our context here, I will make one observation.

Light was an important narrative element in portraying a theophany, an appearing of the LORD to transform human history (18:12). Sunrise marks the beginning of another day of God's handiwork in the created realm. Light is a reminder, then, of God's dominion in both the natural realm and on the historical stage. The lampstands mark the presence of God within Israel. He is clearly seen in what he has made and in what he has done or will do.

Three times in the Psalms God "shines forth" (50:2; 80:1; 94:1). Each time the context is one of vengeance. God will crush the foe. The presence of God will be seen in what he is about to do. "O LORD, the God who avenges, O God who avenges, shine forth. Rise up, O Judge of the earth; pay back to the proud what they deserve" (94:1–2).

The term "glory" (GK 3883) refers first to the holiness of God. "The term *kabod* ('glory') in reference to God normally describes that awesome and innate essence of God that is so intensely 'other' than human

The House of the LORD

experience that it is described as brilliant light or a consuming fire."[1] It refers secondly to a revelation of the presence of God.

As for the LORD's holiness, notice the parallel between "glory" and "splendor of his holiness" in 29:2: "Ascribe to the LORD the glory due his name; worship the LORD in the splendor of his holiness" (see also 79:9; 115:1). "Glorious splendor" characterizes both his majesty (145:5) and his kingdom (145:12; see also 145:11).

Since God took up residence in Zion's temple, it is there that his glory dwells (26:8), and from the perspective of exile, will dwell there again (102:16). He is present there. "His glory dwells in our land" (85:9). If only that presence were manifest throughout the whole world. If only all people could experience the awesome nature of the divine presence! "May the whole earth be filled with his glory" (72:19; see also 97:6; 102:15). "Let your glory be over all the earth" (57:5, 11; 108:5). If only everyone could echo David's words: "I have seen you in the sanctuary and beheld your power and your glory" (63:2).

The glory of the LORD is great (138:5); it endures forever (104:31). This glory prompts song (66:2) and proclamation (29:1; 96:3, 7, 8) as the passions of praise (72:19).

Though the heavens proclaim the glory of the LORD (19:1), and that proclamation is a matter of public record, and though He is exalted beyond the cosmic realm (113:4), the entirety of the human race has yet to submit to his rule and to embrace him in worship.

NEW TESTAMENT PARALLEL

The term "temple" (GK 2639) occurs seventy-two times. All but two uses refer to the Jerusalem Temple complex. Acts 19:27 refers to the Temple of Artemis. First Corinthians 9:13 refers to pagan temples. A second noun for "temple" (GK 3724) occurs forty-five times. This noun generally focuses attention upon the central sanctuary of the temple. For example, Matthew 27:51 refers to the tearing of the interior curtain or veil. Luke 1:9 refers to Zechariah burning incense on the interior altar.

The metaphoric uses of this noun are very compelling. In John 2:21 Jesus refers to his resurrected body as the temple. To speak of a personal resurrection in the midst of time was bold enough, but to suggest then

---

1. Wilson, *Psalms Volume 1*, 362.

that through that resurrected body one had access to the presence of God and forgiveness of sin was audacious.

Paul teaches that the Christian community is the temple of God and God's Spirit dwells in that community. "We are the temple of the living God" (2 Cor 6:16; see also 1 Cor 3:16, 17; 6:19). "In him [Jesus] the whole building is joined together and rises to become a holy temple in the Lord. And in him you too are being built together to become a dwelling in which God lives by his Spirit" (Eph 2:21–22; see also 1 Pet 2:5). This Temple that now is (1 Cor 3:16; 6:19), which is even now in building (Eph 2:19–22), will yet come in all its glorious reality (Rev 21:3).

In the Revelation of John two opposing images are offered, but one compelling truth. Revelation 3:12 offers a physical depiction of the presence of God. "Him who overcomes I will make a pillar in the temple of my God. Never again will he leave it." But Revelation 21:22 banishes any thought of a physical representation of God's presence. God himself is the temple. "I did not see a temple in the city, because the Lord God Almighty and the Lamb are its temple." The believer has a permanent (a pillar in the temple) place in the unrestricted (no temple) presence of God!

~

"If you busy yourself in Psalms, you emerge knowing God." How does one busy oneself in a psalm or in a characteristic of God? You study, you meditate, you sing, and you pray.

MEDITATION

If you were an ancient Israelite, you came to the temple to offer a song of thanksgiving and a thank offering (sacrifice). Read Psalm 66:13–15 and Jonah 2:7–9. You would have offered words of thanks because the Lord had recently delivered you from some trouble or peril. Has the Lord recently delivered you from peril? What are the lyrics of your song of thanksgiving?

If you were an ancient Israelite, you would also journey to the temple to seek asylum. Read Psalm 17:6–9. If you had been denied justice or unjustly persecuted, you went to the house of the Lord to seek vindication from him. Have you recently been denied justice? With what words do you now come to seek his help?

If you were an ancient Israelite, you would also journey to the temple for restoration after recovery from illness. Read Luke 17:14. Have you recently recovered from illness? What are the lyrics of your praise?

If you were an ancient Israelite, you journeyed to the temple to worship the King of kings. Read Psalm 24. How heart-felt is your worship today?

The ancient Israelite came to the temple because he or she "suffered troubles and perils, and faced extreme danger of persecution and slander, of deadly disease and the questioning of his righteousness. The institutions and the psalms that belong with them make it plain that the individual man or woman is helpless, needy, subject to attack by hostile powers. Yahweh is the only hope for better things."[2] Our God is still our only hope!

MUSICAL REFLECTION

William O. Cushing (1823–1902) wrote 300 gospel hymns. "Under His Wings" was inspired by Psalm 17:8—"Hide me in the shadow of your wings."

> Under His wings I am safely abiding; tho the night deepens and tempests are wild, still I can trust Him; I know He will keep me; He has redeemed me, and I am His child.

> Under His wings, what a refuge in sorrow! How the heart yearningly turns to His rest! Often when earth has no balm for my healing, there I find comfort and there I am blest.

> Under His wings, O what precious enjoyment! There will I hide till life's trials are o'er; sheltered, protected, no evil can harm me; resting in Jesus I'm safe evermore.

> Refrain: Under His wings, under His wings, who from His love can sever? Under His wings my soul shall abide, safely abide forever.

PRAYER

Most precious heavenly Father, to be in your presence is both terrifying and comforting. I understand David's longing to be in the house of the Lord, for you were there.

---

2. Kraus, *Theology of the Psalms*, 141.

God, I am so grateful I am alive after the cross. I don't have to go to a physical place to be with you, because I am now a part of your temple. You have said that if I love you and obey your words, you will come and make your dwelling within me.

God, when I felt your glory, I was so fearful of your holiness that I could not move, could not think, and could not breathe. You engulfed me, and then I knew your sovereignty at a deeper level.

It is in your presence God that I worship you with words of praise and adoration. I love you. I am in awe of you, and I lift you high. Let all creation praise you. As I praise you, you lovingly gaze at me, and then I am complete. Totally wrapped in your love, I find rest in you. I experience what I was created for—intimate relationship with you.

Loving Father, I long for all people to hunger after your presence. It is where we all belong. In your holy name, I pray. Amen.

∼

What are your song and your prayer?

13

The Praise of God

> "Sing praises to God, sing praises! Sing praises
> to our King, sing praises!" (Psalm 47:6)

THE VERB "TO BLESS" (GK 1385) occurs seventy-four times. Six times men bless men: 10:3; 49:18; 62:4; 72:15; 118:26; 129:8. The LORD is both subject and object of this verb. That is, the LORD blesses and is blessed. We are comfortable with the idea of the LORD blessing the righteous (5:12; 37:22; 112:2), his people (28:9; 29:11; 67:1, 6, 7; 107:38; 109:28; 115:12 [three times], 13, 15; 118:26a; 128:4–5; 134:3; 147:13), the king (45:2), the land (65:10; 132:15), or even the nations (72:17).

But forty-four times the LORD is the one blessed. That may sound heretical to some. Since the LORD is complete and perfect in himself, he lacks nothing which a blessing may add. In fact, in these instances the NIV has translated this verb either "to praise" or "to extol." But the Hebrew literally says "bless." Gerald Wilson understands correctly: "The Israelites understood that grateful humans desire to give to God something more than laudatory praise, and that is what blessing is all about—the desire to heap good and benefit on the one blessed."[1]

Not surprisingly, when we "bless" the LORD, we are mindful of how he has blessed us. Let me illustrate this by isolating the seventeen occurrences where a passive participle ("be blessed") of the verb is in usage. The NIV consistently translates this "Praise be to the LORD" (113:2 is the exception).

---

1. Wilson, *Psalms Volume 1*, 311.

"Praise be to my Rock! Exalted be God my Savior!	He is the God who avenges me, who subdues nations under me, who saves me from my enemies" (18:46–48a).
"Praise be to the LORD,	for he has heard my cry for mercy" (28:6).
"Praise be to the LORD,	for he showed his wonderful love to me when I was in a besieged city" (31:21).
"Praise be to the LORD, the God of Israel, from everlasting to everlasting. Amen and Amen" (41:13).	This verse concludes Book One. This doxology is a fitting conclusion to a book which celebrates all that the LORD has done.
"Praise be to God,	who has not rejected my prayer or withheld his love from me!" (66:20).
"Praise be to the Lord, to God, our Savior,	who daily bears our burdens" (68:19).
Praise be to God" (68:35).	"You are awesome, O God, in your sanctuary; the God of Israel gives power and strength to his people.
"Praise be to the LORD God, the God of Israel,	who alone does marvelous deeds" (72:18).
"Praise be to his glorious name forever; may the whole earth be filled with his glory. Amen and Amen" (72:19).	This verse concludes Book Two. Like 41:13 this doxology is also a fitting conclusion.
"Praise be to the LORD forever! Amen and Amen" (89:52).	This verse concludes Book Three. Like 41:13 and 72:19, this doxology is also a fitting conclusion.
"Praise be to the LORD, the God of Israel, from everlasting to everlasting. Let all the people say, 'Amen!'" (106:48).	This verse concludes Book Four. Like 41:13; 72:19; and 89:52, it is also a fitting conclusion.
"Let the name of the LORD be praised, both now and forevermore....	He raises the poor from the dust and lifts the needy from the ash heap; he seats them with princes, with the princes of their people. He settles the barren woman in her home as a happy mother of children" (113:2, 7–9).
"Praise be to you, O LORD,	teach me your decrees" (119:12).
"Praise be to the LORD,	who has not let us be torn by their teeth" (124:6).
"Praise be to the LORD from Zion,	to him who dwells in Jerusalem" (135:21).
"Praise be to the LORD my Rock,	who trains my hands for war, my fingers for battle" (144:1).

The Praise of God

The verb "to praise" (GK 2146) appears eighty-nine times. In all but five (10:3; 49:6; 52:1; 78:63; 97:7), the LORD is the object of praise. The LORD is worthy of praise (18:3; 48:1; 96:4; 113:3; 145:3). Heaven and earth praise him (69:34; 148:1). The heavens include the "highest heavens" (148:4); sun, moon, and stars (148:3); waters above the skies (148:4); and the angelic host (148:2). The earth includes the sea and its great creatures (148:7); mountains and trees (148:9); wild and domesticated animals (148:10); birds (148:10); kings and commoners (148:11–12). The human voice (63:5; 69:30) is accompanied by dancing (149:3) and orchestration—trumpet, harp, lyre, strings, flute, and cymbals (149:3; 150:3–5).[2]

The poor and the needy praise the LORD (74:21). All the upright praise him (64:10), as do those who seek (22:26) and fear the LORD (22:23). The servants of the LORD praise him (135:1). He is praised in his mighty heavens (148:1; 150:1), amongst the nations (117:1), in Zion (147:12), in the congregation (22:22; 35:18; 109:30), in the council of the elders (107:32), and in the psalmist's soul (146:1).

He is praised every day (145:2), yea, even seven times a day (119:164). He is praised throughout a lifetime (119:175; 146:2), now and forevermore (113:2; 115:18). He is praised in eternity.

Our blessing and praise of God express our delight in Him. Amazingly, God delights in us. The verb "be pleased with, accept favorably" (GK 8354) appears thirteen times in the Psalter. Nine times God is the subject of the verb. Because the LORD was pleased with his people, that is, he loved them, he triumphed over their enemies in capturing the Promised Land. The LORD takes delight in his people by crowning them with salvation (149:4). He delights in those who fear him (147:11; compare 147:10). He does not delight in empty ritual (51:16), but in humble and heartfelt sincerity (51:17; 119:108). Because the LORD has shown favor in the past (85:1), the psalmists can ask him to show his good pleasure again (40:13; 77:7).

The noun "favor" (GK 8356) appears thirteen times as well. The LORD surrounds the righteous with his favor (5:12). "Remember me, O LORD, when you show favor to your people, come to my aid when

---

2. "The purpose of singing and playing was to please Yahweh. Whether in the personal song of thanksgiving or in the many-voiced choir, one sang and played before Yahweh, for Yahweh (Pss. 71:22; 104:33; 138:1; 144:9)." Keel, *The Symbolism of the Biblical World: Ancient Near Eastern Iconography and the Book of Psalms*, 351.

you save them" (106:4). The LORD's favor exalts Israel's king (89:17) and Israel's capital, Jerusalem (51:18). This favor lasts a lifetime (30:5) and provides an unshakeable security (30:7) and a sure basis for prayer (69:13). The LORD shows his favor by satisfying and fulfilling the desires of those who fear him (145:16, 19). Our meditation (19:14) and devotion to the LORD's will (40:8; 103:21; 143:10) are pleasing to him.

The verb "delight in" (GK 2911) occurs seventeen times. When God is the subject of the verb, four ideas are to be found. First, God is free to do whatever pleases him (115:3; 135:6). Second, God is pleased with sincerity and integrity (51:6), but not with an empty show of sacrifice (40:6; 51:16; but see 51:19) or of strength (147:10). Third, since God delights in his people, he rescues or delivers them from the foe (18:19; 22:8). "I know that you are pleased with me, for my enemy does not triumph over me" (41:11). Fourth, there will be ups and downs in life, but God is a steadying presence. "If the LORD delights in a man's way, he makes his steps firm; though he stumble, he will not fall, for the LORD upholds him with his hand" (37:23-24).

When man is the subject of the verb, one prominent thought is found. The psalmists desire either the LORD himself (73:25) or his word (40:8; 112:1; 119:35).

The noun "blessing" (GK 1388) occurs only eight times in the Psalter. David prays, "May your blessing be on your people" (3:8; see also 129:8). The kings of Israel experienced rich (21:3) and eternal (21:6) blessings from the LORD. Those who seek the LORD receive blessing from the LORD (24:5; 37:26). "When brothers live together in unity" (133:1), "the LORD bestows his blessing" (133:3; contrast 109:17).

The verb "to give thanks, laud, praise" (GK 3344) occurs sixty-seven times. Often the psalmists explain their reason for praise or thanksgiving. The verb is followed by the particle, ki, pronounced *key*, and often translated "for" or "because." "I will praise" the LORD because of...." "We give thanks, for...." The keys to thanksgiving are:

"Praise the LORD with the harp...	For the word of the LORD is right and true; he is faithful in all he does" (33:2, 4).
"I will praise you forever	for what you have done" (52:9a; see also 105:1; 111:1-2).

"I will praise your name, O LORD,	for it is good" (54:6; see also 30:4; 44:8; 97:12; 99:3; 122:4).
"I will praise you, O Lord my God, with all my heart (see also 9:1a; 138:1a); I will glorify your name forever.	For great is your love toward me; you have delivered me from the depths of the grave" (86:12-13).
"It is good to praise the LORD and make music to your name, O Most High …	For you make me glad by your deeds, O LORD" (92:1, 4).
"Give thanks to the LORD,	for he is good; his love endures forever" (106:1; 107:1; 118:1, 29; 136:1; see also 100:4-5).
"I will praise you, O LORD, among the nations; I will sing of you among the peoples.	For great is your love, higher than the heavens; your faithfulness reaches to the skies" (108:3-4; see also 57:9-10).
"With my mouth I will greatly extol the LORD; in the great throng I will praise him.	For he stands at the right hand of the needy one, to save his life from those who condemn him" (109:30-31; 140:12-13).
"I will give you thanks,	for you answered me; you have become my salvation" (118:21).
"Give thanks to the God of gods,	for his love endures forever" (136:2, 3, 36).
"I praise you	because I am fearfully and wonderfully made" (139:14).

Many times context offers the content of thanksgiving. "I will give thanks to the LORD because of his *righteousness*" (7:17; see also 118:19). "At midnight I rise to give you thanks for your *righteous laws*" (119:62; see also 119:7; 138:4). "I will praise you with the harp for your *faithfulness*" (71:22; see also 89:5; 138:2). "Let them give thanks to the LORD for his *unfailing love* and his wonderful deeds for men" (107:8, 15, 21, 31). "We give thanks to you, O God, we give thanks, for *your Name is near*" (75:1). "*Save* us, O LORD our God, and gather us from the nations, that we may give thanks to your holy name and glory in your praise" (106:47; see also 18:48-49; 28:6-7; 35:17-18). "*Set me free* from prison, that I may praise your name" (142:7). "Surely your *wrath* against men brings you praise" (76:10; see also 79:12-13). "*You are my God*, and I will give you thanks" (118:28).

This praise or thanksgiving will be international in its voice. "May the peoples praise you, O God; may all the peoples praise you" (67:3, 5; see also 45:17; 145:10).

The noun (GK 9343) related to this verb is variously translated: praise (26:7), thanksgiving (42:4; 69:30; 95:2; 100:4; 147:7), and thank offerings (50:14, 23; 56:12; 107:22; 116:17). Psalm 100 is a psalm for "giving thanks." "Enter his gates with thanksgiving and his courts with praise; give thanks to him and praise his name. For the LORD is good and his love endures forever; his faithfulness continues through all generations" (100:4–5).

Seven different verbs are used to express the idea "to rejoice." (1) "rejoice, be glad" occurs fifty-two times (GK 8523); (2) "give a ringing cry" occurs twenty-five times (GK 8264); (3) "rejoice" occurs nineteen times (GK 1635); (4) "raise a shout" occurs 12 times (GK 8131); (5) "exult, rejoice" occurs seven times (GK 8464); (6) "exult" occurs seven times (GK 6600); and (7) "rejoice, exult" occurs four times (GK 6636). Here are example verses for each of these seven verbs:

1. "In him our hearts *rejoice*, for we trust in his holy name" (33:21).
2. "For you make me glad by your deeds, O LORD; I *sing for joy* at the works of your hands" (92:4).
3. "My heart *rejoices* in your salvation" (13:5).
4. "Come, let us sing for joy to the LORD; let us *shout aloud* to the Rock of our salvation" (95:1).
5. "May all who seek you *rejoice* and be glad in you" (40:16; 70:4).
6. "The LORD is my strength and my shield; my heart trusts in him, and I am helped. My heart *leaps for joy* and I will give thanks to him in song" (28:7).
7. "I will be glad and *rejoice* in you; I will sing praise to your name, O Most High" (9:2).

Using verb #1 above, the following are reasons why we rejoice: Rejoice because the LORD reigns (96:10–11; 97:1). Rejoice because his unfailing love surrounds the man or woman who trusts in him (32:10–11; see also 90:14). Rejoice in his strength (21:1). Rejoice in his deeds (92:4). Rejoice in his works on man's behalf (66:5). Rejoice that he is our refuge

(5:11; 64:10). Rejoice that he revives us (85:6). Rejoice because he rules or judges justly (67:4). Rejoice when he turns back our enemies (9:2–3). Rejoice when the LORD restores the fortunes of his people (14:7; 53:6). Rejoice in the Word of the LORD (19:8). Rejoice in God (63:11). Rejoice when he avenges you (58:10). Rejoice in worship (122:1). Rejoice in the day the LORD has made (118:24). Rejoice in our Maker (149:2). Rejoice in seeking the one who may be found (40:16; 70:4; 105:3). Rejoice because he knows the anguish of our souls (31:7). Rejoice because he lifts the needy out of affliction (107:41). Rejoice because he is at your right hand (16:8). Rejoice in his holy Name (33:21).

The act of "lifting up the hands" to God is a gesture of prayer, whether it be supplication (28:2; 141:2), praise (63:4; 134:2), or meditation (119:48). [God lifts his hand to take an oath (106:26) or to extend help to the needy (10:12; see also 91:12)]. When the psalmists "lift up the soul" to the LORD, they are offering their absolute loyalty to him alone (25:1; 86:4 [note the word "servant"]; 143:8). By contrast, one may lift up one's soul to "emptiness," a word the NIV translates "idol" (24:4; see also 139:20). Shall we offer our devotion to the LORD or to a false god?

The verb "be high, exalted" (GK 8123) occurs fifty-one times in the Psalter. When God is the subject of the verb, he raises up or lifts the psalmist from some miserable condition. "O LORD, see how my enemies persecute me! Have mercy and lift me up from the gates of death" (9:13). "You exalted me above my foes; from violent men you rescued me" (18:48b). "He raises the poor from the dust and lifts the needy from the ash heap" (113:7). God also raised up or "established" David and his dynasty and kept them safe (27:5–6; 89:17, 19, 24; 92:10; 112:9; 148:14). Only God can exalt a man (75:6–7).

When man is the subject of the verb, he exalts or praises God. "I will exalt you, O LORD, for you lifted me out of the depths and did not let my enemies gloat over me" (30:1). "Glorify the LORD with me; let us exalt his name together" (34:3; see also 18:46; 99:5, 9; 107:32; 118:28; 145:1).

A number of verses speak of the LORD as exalted, a status befitting his eternal and righteous rule. "The LORD is exalted over all the nations" (113:4). "I will be exalted among the nations, I will be exalted in the earth" (46:10). "Be exalted, O God, above the heavens" (57:5a, 11a; 108:5; see also 89:13b; 118:16; 138:6).

Our praise of God is often accompanied by musical instrumentation. The Hebrew noun translated "harp" occurs eight times (33:2; 57:8;

71:22; 81:2; 92:3; 108:2; 144:9; 150:3). "I will praise you with the harp for your faithfulness, O my God; I will sing praise to you with the lyre, O Holy One of Israel" (71:22). The noun "lyre" (though it is often translated "harp" by NIV) occurs fourteen times. Tambourine appears four times (68:25; 81:2; 149:3; 150:4); trumpets (two types; one being the famous shophar, the ram's horn) five times (47:5; 81:3; 98:6; 150:3); cymbals twice (150:5); flute once (150:4); and strings once (150:4).

The noun "peoples" (GK 6639) occurs thirty-eight times. Two major ideas revolve around this word. First, the LORD judges the peoples (7:8; 67:4) in truth (96:13) and with equity (96:10; 98:9). God may judge peoples by subduing them. "He subdued nations under us, peoples under our feet" (47:3; see also 18:47; 45:5). In anger the LORD brings down peoples (56:7), who tremble or quake before him (99:1). "You are the God who performs miracles; you display your power among the peoples" (77:14). God may judge the peoples by thwarting their purposes (33:10; 68:30) and turning aside their taunts (89:50–51).

Second, God's people proclaim Him among the peoples, who, in turn, worship him. "Declare his glory among the nations, his marvelous deeds among all peoples" (96:3). "Make known among the peoples what he has done" (105:1; see also 9:11; 49:1). "I will praise you, O LORD, among the nations; I will sing of you among the peoples" (57:9; 108:3). Because of this proclamation, the peoples praise or worship the LORD. "Praise our God, O peoples, let the sound of his praise be heard" (66:8). "I will perpetuate your memory through all generations; therefore the peoples will praise you for ever and ever" (45:17; see also 47:1, 9; 67:3, 5; 87:6; 96:7; 97:6; 102:22).

"Great is the LORD in Zion; he is exalted over all the peoples. Let them praise your great and awesome name—he is holy" (99:2–3).

NEW TESTAMENT PARALLEL

In the New Testament the verb "give praise, honor" (δοξάζω = doxazō; GK 1519) occurs sixty-one times. The gospels often note that the crowds praised God after Jesus had performed a miraculous healing. Matthew 15:31 illustrates the point: "The people were amazed when they saw the mute speaking, the crippled made well, the lame walking and the blind seeing. And they praised the God of Israel."

People praised God when Jesus healed a paralytic (Matt 9:8; Mark 2:12; Luke 5:25–26), a crippled woman (Luke 13:13), a leper (Luke 17:15), and a blind beggar (Luke 18:43). People praised God when Jesus brought back to life the widow's son in Nain (Luke 7:16) and Lazarus (John 11:4). When Peter and John, disciples of Jesus, also healed a crippled beggar, the people praised God (Acts 4:21).

These wondrous displays of Jesus' love and power brought praise or glory to the Father (John 14:13; 17:4). The common Greek noun for glory (δόξα = doxa; GK 1518) is the stem of the verb under review here, as you can see.

Early Christians praised God when Saul was converted to Christ and commissioned to share the good news of the gospel with the Gentiles (Gal 1:24). Early Christians praised God when Paul (formerly known as Saul) shared that message and the Gentiles believed in Jesus (Acts 21:20; see also 11:18; Rom 15:9).

We continue to praise God for the teaching of Jesus (Luke 4:15) and for the life he lived (Luke 23:47). People will continue to praise God for obedience to the gospel of Christ and for generous mercy extended in his name (2 Cor 9:13). We will praise God for the gifts of the Holy Spirit at work in the body of Christ (1 Pet 4:11). We will praise God for the honor of bearing the name of Christ, even if it means suffering for our Lord (1 Pet 4:16).

The noun "psalm" (GK 6011) occurs seven times. Four times it refers to the Book of Psalms (Luke 20:42; 24:44; Acts 1:20) or some psalm therein (Acts 13:33). Three times it refers to a psalm or hymn of praise (1 Cor 14:26; Eph 5:19; Col 3:16). The noun "hymn" (GK 5631) appears just two times (Eph 5:19; Col 3:16). The noun "song" (GK 6046) occurs seven times in the New Testament. Christians speak to one another with "spiritual songs" (Eph 5:19; Col 3:16). New songs are sung in Revelation (5:9; 14:3; 15:3) to honor the victory of the Lamb.

The verb "to lift or raise up, to exalt, uplift" occurs twenty times in the New Testament. Twice in Acts we read that God exalted Jesus to his own right hand (2:33; 5:31). This exaltation or lifting up came because Jesus submitted himself to death by crucifixion, a lifting up unto death (John 3:14; 8:28; 12:32–24).

This pattern—whoever humbles himself will be exalted—characterizes the Christian walk (James 4:10; 1 Pet 5:6), Christian repentance (Luke 18:14), Christian ministry to the disadvantaged (Luke 14:11), and Christian proclamation (2 Cor 11:7). The reverse—whoever exalts himself will be humbled—was evident when Capernaum was debased (Matt 11:23; Luke 10:15).

God has lifted up the humble, and he will continue to do so. Mary sang this (Luke 1:52); Jesus' exaltation proved this; and our future glorification hopes in this.

∼

"If you busy yourself in Psalms, you emerge knowing God." How does one busy oneself in a psalm or in a characteristic of God? You study, you meditate, you sing, and you pray.

MEDITATION

- Blessing is the desire to give. If you desire to bless God, what would you give him?
- For what are you thankful? Is it easy for you to be grateful?
- Why do you suppose there are so many different Hebrew words for "praise"? How many are in your vocabulary list?
- The Psalms are mission-minded. Are you? Are we? Is your church?

C. S. Lewis once wrote, "I think we delight to praise what we enjoy because the praise not merely expresses but completes the enjoyment; it is its appointed consummation. It is not out of compliment that lovers keep on telling one another how beautiful they are; the delight is incomplete till it is expressed."[3]

Do you delight in God? Have you praised Him and thus consummated the delight? In commanding us to praise Him, God is inviting us to enjoy Him. Do you believe that? Do we live it?

MUSICAL REFLECTION

Despite becoming blind shortly after birth, Frances "Fanny" Jane Crosby (1820–1915) penned approximately 8,000 hymns. In 1869 she wrote the following words for the hymn "Praise Him! Praise Him!"

> Praise Him! Praise Him! Jesus, our blessed Redeemer!
> Sing, O Earth, His wonderful love proclaim!
> Hail Him! hail Him! highest archangels in glory;
> Strength and honor give to His holy Name!

---

3. Lewis, *Reflections on the Psalms*, 95.

The Praise of God

Like a shepherd, Jesus will guard His children,
In His arms He carries them all day long:

Refrain
Praise Him! Praise Him!
Tell of His excellent greatness.
Praise Him! Praise Him!
Ever in joyful song!

Praise Him! Praise Him! Jesus, our blessed Redeemer!
For our sins He suffered, and bled, and died.
He our Rock, our hope of eternal salvation,
Hail Him! hail Him! Jesus the Crucified.
Sound His praises! Jesus who bore our sorrows,
Love unbounded, wonderful, deep and strong.
Refrain

Praise Him! Praise Him! Jesus, our blessed Redeemer!
Heav'nly portals loud with hosannas ring!
Jesus, Savior, reigneth forever and ever.
Crown Him! Crown Him! Prophet, and Priest, and King!
Christ is coming! over the world victorious,
Pow'r and glory unto the Lord belong.
Refrain

PRAYER

God, my God, my soul rejoices in you. My being longs to bless you for your acts of love. You have saved me from death, giving me life everlasting. I long to praise you because you have given to me my worth and my identity. You, who are infinitely powerful, want to have an intimate relationship with me. How awesome! How incredible! Bless your name forever. Exalted be God, my Savior.

Sometimes, God, I am frustrated by my lack of words to adequately praise you. That is why I have spoken with groans that only your Spirit understands. You understand my spirit. I thank you.

I can hardly wait to praise you with the throng of ten thousand angels. O that my voice would join the symphony of praise and blessing.

I understand why David states that the heavens, the highest heavens, the sun, moon, and stars, the earth, its great creatures, the mountains and the trees, animals, kings and commoners all praise you. It's as if he wants all of creation to join his voice in praise. His voice is not enough. All should praise you. O that all would worship you!

You are exalted, O Most High God. Praise his holy name, O my soul. All that is within me blesses the Almighty God, my Savior.

∼

What are your song and your prayer?

Bibliography

Ackroyd, Peter R. *Doors of Perception: A Guide to Reading the Psalms*. London: SCM, 1983.
Allen, Leslie C. *Psalms 101-150*. Word Biblical Commentary. Waco, Texas: Word, 1983.
Bullock, C. Hassell. *Encountering the Book of Psalms*. Grand Rapids: Baker, 2001.
Chisholm, Robert B. "A Theology of the Psalms." In *A Biblical Theology of the Old Testament*, 257-304. Chicago: Moody, 1991.
Craigie, Peter C. *Psalms 1-50*. Word Biblical Commentary. Waco, Texas: Word, 1983.
Delitzsch, Franz. *Psalms*. Commentary on the Old Testament in Ten Volumes. Grand Rapids: Eerdmans, 1980.
Fee, Gordon D., and Douglas Stuart. *How to Read the Bible for All Its Worth*. Grand Rapids: Zondervan, 1993.
Firth, David, and Philip S. Johnston. *Interpreting the Psalms: Issues and Approaches*. Downers Grove, IL: InterVarsity, 2005.
Futato, Mark D. *Interpreting the Psalms: An Exegetical Handbook*. Handbooks for Old Testament Exegesis. Grand Rapids: Kregel, 2007.
Goodrick, Edward W., and John R. Kohlenberger III. *Zondervan NIV Exhaustive Concordance*. 2nd ed. Grand Rapids: Zondervan, 1999.
Holladay, William L. *The Psalms through Three Thousand Years*. Minneapolis: Fortress, 1996.
Keel, Othmar. *The Symbolism of the Biblical World: Ancient Near Eastern Iconography and the Book of Psalms*. Translated by Timothy J. Hallett. Winona Lake, IN: Eisenbrauns, 1997.
Kidner, Derek. *Psalms 1-72*. Tyndale Old Testament Commentaries. Downers Grove, IL: InterVarsity, 1973.
———. *Psalms 73-150*. Tyndale Old Testament Commentaries. Downers Grove, IL: InterVarsity, 1975.
Kraus, Hans-Joachim. *Theology of the Psalms*. Translated by Keith Crim. Minneapolis: Augsburg, 1986.
Lewis, C. S. *Reflections on the Psalms*. New York: Harcourt Brace Jovanovich, 1958.
Longman, Tremper III. *How to Read the Psalms*. Downers Grove, IL: InterVarsity, 1988.
Mays, James L. *The Lord Reigns: A Theological Handbook to the Psalms*. Louisville: John Knox, 1994.
Tate, Marvin E. *Psalms 51-100*. Word Biblical Commentary. Waco, TX: Word, 1990.
Willard, Dallas. *The Divine Conspiracy*. San Francisco: Harper, 1998.
Wilson, Gerald H. *Psalms Volume 1*. The New Application Commentary. Grand Rapids: Zondervan, 2002.

Scripture Index

Genesis
1:1   24
12:3   10, 20
14:19   20, 21
14:20   20
14:22   21
15:13–16   10
17:2   10
20:7   34
22:16–18   10
32:28   10
49:18   58
49:24   10

Exodus
3:6   10
3:15   8, 10
4:5   10
15:3–4a   52
19:5   14
23:14–17   103
25:10   20, 105
25:11   105
25:19   105
25:20   105
30:10   62
34:6   94
34:10   18
34:29–35   99

Numbers
6:25   99
14:18   94
18:20   13

Deuteronomy
4:15–16   92
7:6   14
14:2   14
17:18–20   35
26:18   14
28:4   86
32:10–11   49

Joshua
10:11   29
10:14   52–53

Judges
8:10–11   36
8:23   33

1 Samuel
4:4   19
16:11   84
16:19   84
17:15   84
17:20   84
17:34–37   84
22:4   55
22:5   55
24:22   55

2 Samuel
5:7   55
5:9   55
5:17   55
6:15   19

7:7–8   84
7:8   14
7:11b–12   34
7:14   14
7:18   43
15:4   38
23:1   10
23:14   55

1 Kings
1:50   62
2:2b–3   35
2:28   62
7:49   106

2 Kings
6:8–23   36
19:22   11

1 Chronicles
28:2   98
29:3   14

2 Chronicles
9:18   98
17:8   71

Nehemiah
2:10   71
4:5   88
7:62   71
9:17   94

Job

25:2	17

Psalms

2:1–2	43
2:2	33, 34, 38
2:4	12, 44
2:6	33, 34, 41
2:8	14
2:10	33, 34, 79
2:12	47
3:3	43, 51, 52
3:6	21, 51
3:7	40
3:8	60, 114
4:1	2, 61, 93, 95
4:2	3
4:5	85
4:6	27, 71, 99
4:6b	13
5:2	2, 33, 34, 36
5:4	106
5:5	72
5:7	42, 72, 103, 104
5:8	76, 87
5:9	95
5:11	9, 47, 117
5:12	52, 111, 113
6:2	61
6:3	3
6:4	59
6:4b	72
6:5	29
6:6–7	3
7:1–2	47
7:1	47
7:2	48
7:6	40, 41
7:8	79, 118
7:9	76, 80, 94
7:10	52, 59
7:11	76, 79
7:17	9, 11, 115
8:1	9, 12, 13, 24, 44
8:3	24, 25, 44, 97
8:4–8	96
8:5–6	24
8:5	39
8:6	24, 25, 42
8:9	9, 12, 13
9:1	26, 115
9:2–3	117
9:2	9, 11, 116
9:3	26
9:4	38, 79
9:5	8, 88
9:7	38, 73, 81
9:8	79, 81
9:9	54
9:10	9, 65, 85
9:11	41, 118
9:13	61, 92, 93, 117
9:14	41, 60
9:19–20	40
9:19	40, 79
10:1	3
10:3	111, 113
10:4	94
10:9	48
10:10	26
10:11	100
10:12	40, 97, 117
10:14	39, 92, 93, 97
10:15	97
10:16	33, 34, 36, 73
10:17	93
10:18	39, 79
11:1	47
11:4–5	80
11:4	38, 44, 92, 104
11:5	72
11:6	80
11:7	76, 80, 99
12:4	29, 86
12:7	62
13:1–2	3
13:2	100
13:3	95, 100
13:5–6	60
13:5	71, 85, 116
14:1	71
14:2	44, 93
14:3	71
14:6	47
14:7	10, 27, 41, 60, 117
15:1	29, 105, 106
15:2	77, 106
15:3	87, 103
15:5	55
16:1	47, 62
16:2	12, 71
16:3	13
16:4	8
16:5	13
16:6	14
16:7	94
16:8	55, 97, 117
16:11	97
17:1	2, 48, 93
17:2	81, 92
17:3	80
17:6–9	108
17:6	2, 48, 93
17:7–9	48–49
17:7	47, 59, 71, 97
17:8	100, 105, 109
17:10–12	49
17:12	47, 48
17:13–14	49
17:13	40, 58
17:14	97
17:15	99
18	42, 93, 98
18:1	62
18:2	47, 52, 53, 54, 58, 62
18:3	113
18:6	93, 104
18:8	94

Scripture Index

Psalms (cont.)					
18:9	98	21:8	97	25:2	85
18:10	105	21:13	3, 25	25:3	63
18:12	106	22:1	3	25:4–5a	78
18:13	11, 44	22:2	95	25:5	63
18:15	94, 96	22:3	11	25:6	61, 71, 73
18:17	60	22:4	58, 85	25:7	61, 70, 72, 80, 89
18:19	114	22:5	85	25:8	70, 80
18:27	59	22:8	58, 114	25:10	73, 77
18:30	47, 52	22:9	85	25:11	9, 88
18:31	9, 27, 53	22:11	87, 89	25:12	29
18:34	97	22:12	48	25:13	71
18:35	51, 52, 97	22:13	47, 48	25:16	61
18:41	95	22:15	49	25:18	88, 92, 93
18:43	58	22:16	48	25:19–20	47–48
18:46–48a	112	22:19	89	25:19	92, 93
18:46	13, 54, 117	22:20	48	25:20	47, 62
18:47	118	22:21	48, 62	25:21	63
18:48–49	115	22:22	9, 113	26:1	79
18:48	58, 60, 117	22:23	10, 113	26:2–3	80
18:49	9	22:24	100	26:2	85, 94
18:50	35, 38, 60, 71	22:26	65, 113	26:3	72, 78
18:51	33	22:27	42	26:6	106
19:1	24, 25, 96, 107	22:28	41, 42	26:7	116
19:4–6	25	22:29	43	26:8	54, 103, 104, 106, 107
19:8	80, 100, 117	22:30	12	26:11	61
19:9	78	22:31	77	26:12	81
19:12	28	23:1	84	27:1–2	14
19:13	42, 89	23:2	84, 87	27:1	13, 21, 27, 54
19:14	53, 60, 114	23:3	9, 87	27:3	21, 85
20:1	9, 10	23:4	21, 84, 86	27:4	6, 65, 103–4, 104
20:2	41, 53	23:6	71, 72, 104	27:5–6	117
20:5	9, 60	24	109	27:5	53, 100, 105
20:6	26, 35, 38, 44, 59, 95, 97	24:3	29	27:6	3, 105
20:7	9	24:4–6	29	27:7	2, 61, 93, 95
20:9	33, 35, 59	24:4	117	27:8	65, 99
21:1	33, 35, 60, 85, 116	24:5–6	65, 77	27:9	100
21:3	39, 71, 114	24:5	114	27:11	81, 87
21:5	35, 60, 68	24:6	10, 99	27:13	13, 70
21:6	114	24:7	33, 34	27:14	63
21:7	11, 33, 35, 55, 71, 85	24:8	25, 27, 33, 34, 36, 40, 53	28:1	53, 95
		24:9	33, 34	28:2	2, 93, 117
		24:10	27, 33, 34, 40		
		25:1	117		

Scripture Index

Psalms (cont.)

28:5	25, 96	32:4	97	35:3	52, 60
28:6–7	115	32:5	88	35:5	42
28:6	112	32:6	2	35:6	42
28:7	2, 52, 85, 116	32:7	58	35:9	60
28:8	38, 54, 60, 85	32:10–11	116	35:10	28, 60, 77
28:9	14, 59, 84, 85, 111	32:10	71, 85	35:12	71
29:1	107	33:2	114, 117	35:17–18	115
29:2	9, 107	33:3	2	35:17	3, 12, 48, 93
29:3–9	25	33:4	25, 78, 80, 114	35:18	26, 113
29:4	26	33:5	71, 76	35:22	12, 89, 93, 95
29:9	104	33:6	24, 44, 94, 96	35:23	12, 41
29:10	33, 34, 36, 73	33:8	21	35:24	79
29:11	85, 111	33:9	24	36	42
30	104	33:10	118	36:5	44, 71, 78
30:1	117	33:11	73, 99	36:6	77
30:4	8, 115	33:12	14	36:7	47, 105
30:5	114	33:13	44	36:8	104
30:5b	4	33:15	99	36:9	13
30:6	55	33:16	33, 34, 35, 59	36:10	77
30:7	100, 114	33:17	59	37:3	71, 78, 84, 85
30:8	12, 61	33:18	63, 71, 92	37:5	85
30:9	78	33:19	60	37:6	13
30:10	2, 61, 93	33:20	52, 53	37:12	48
30:11	4	33:21	8, 9, 85, 99, 116, 117	37:13	12
31:1	47, 58, 77	33:22	63, 71	37:14	48
31:2	53, 54, 93	34:3	9, 117	37:17	97
31:3	9, 53, 54, 87	34:4	60, 66	37:18	14
31:4	54	34:5	99	37:21	61
31:5	77, 97	34:7	42	37:22	111
31:6	85	34:8	47, 70, 95	37:23–24	114
31:7	92, 117	34:9	21	37:24	97
31:7a	72	34:10	21, 66, 71	37:26	61, 114
31:9	61	34:12	29, 71	37:27	71
31:14	85	34:14	29, 65, 71	37:28	63, 73
31:15	60, 97	34:15	92, 93	37:32–33	79
31:16	59, 72, 99	34:16	99	37:39	54, 59
31:19	47, 70	34:17	60	37:40	47, 58
31:20	100	34:18	59, 87	38:2	97
31:21	72, 112	34:19–20	62	38:9	12
31:24	63	34:19	60	38:10	13
32:1	88	34:22	42, 48	38:11	87
32:2	89	35:1	52	38:15	12, 63
		35:2	40, 51, 52	38:20	71
				38:21	89

Scripture Index

Psalms (cont.)

Reference	Pages
38:22	12, 60
39:2	71
39:6	29
39:7	12, 63
39:8	60
39:10	97
39:12	2, 86, 93, 95
40:1–2	53
40:1	63
40:2	63
40:3	21
40:4	85
40:5	25, 26
40:6	114
40:8	114
40:10	60, 72, 77, 78, 79
40:11	62, 72, 78
40:13	113
40:16	60, 66, 116, 117
40:17	12, 58
41:2	62
41:4	61
41:5	3, 8
41:9	85
41:10	61
41:11	114
41:13	6, 10, 73, 112
42–83	9
42:2	3, 13, 99
42:4	103, 104, 116
42:5	4, 60, 63
42:8	4, 86
42:9	53
42:11	60, 63
43:1	58, 79
43:2	4, 54
43:3	13, 78, 87, 104, 106
43:4	106
43:5	60, 63
44:2	96–97
44:3	13, 59, 97, 99
44:4	10, 33, 34, 60
44:5–7	36
44:5	9
44:6–7	59
44:6	85
44:8	9, 115
44:9	4, 39
44:11	86
44:20	8
44:22	86
44:23	4, 12, 41
44:24	100
44:25	49
44:26	40, 72
45:1	33, 35
45:2	35, 111
45:4	19, 77
45:5	33, 35, 118
45:6	38, 39, 73
45:7	81
45:8	104
45:9	33
45:11	33, 35
45:13	33, 34, 35
45:14	33, 35
45:15	33, 35, 104
45:17	9, 116, 118
46	56
46:1	47, 85
46:2–3	86
46:2	21
46:4	11, 41, 104
46:6–7	36
46:6	86
46:7	10, 40, 54, 86
46:9	40
46:10	117
46:11	10, 40, 54, 86
47	19–21
47:1	17, 118
47:2–5	20
47:2	11, 17, 19, 20, 33, 34, 36, 41, 69
47:3–4	20
47:3	118
47:4	10, 14
47:5	118
47:6	3, 19, 20, 33, 34, 111
47:7–9	20, 69
47:7	20, 33, 34, 36, 41
47:8	20, 36, 38, 41
47:9	10, 20, 51, 52, 118
48:1	41, 68, 113
48:2	33, 34, 36, 41
48:4–7	34
48:4	33, 40, 54
48:7	40
48:8	40, 41
48:9	72, 104
48:10	9, 97
48:11	41
48:12	41
49:1	118
49:5	21
49:6	85, 113
49:11	8
49:14	86
49:18	111
49:19	13
50:2	41, 106
50:3	95
50:4	79, 95
50:5	73, 79
50:6	79, 95
50:7	2, 93, 95
50:14	11, 116
50:21	95
50:22	9
50:23	116
51:1	61, 72, 88
51:2	89

Psalms (cont.)

51:4	79
51:6	78, 114
51:7	89
51:9	88, 100
51:11	95
51:14	59, 60
51:15	12, 77
51:16	113, 114
51:17	113
51:18	41, 114
51:19	106, 114
52:1	113
52:3	71
52:5	13
52:7	54, 85
52:8	71, 85, 104
52:9	8, 9, 63, 70, 114
53:1	71
53:2	44, 93
53:3	71
53:6	10, 27, 41, 60, 117
54:1	9, 26, 59, 79
54:2	2, 93
54:4	12
54:5	78
54:6	8, 9, 70, 115
54:7	60
55:1	2, 4
55:2	95
55:9	12
55:14	103, 104
55:20	72
55:22	73
55:23	85
56:1	61
56:3	21, 85
56:4	85
56:7	58, 118
56:11	21, 85
56:12	116
56:13	13, 60
57:1	47, 50, 61, 105, 106
57:2–3	21
57:2	11
57:3	50, 72, 78
57:4	47, 48, 50
57:5	44, 50, 107, 117
57:7–10	50
57:7	3
57:8	40, 117
57:9–10	115
57:9	12, 118
57:10	44, 50, 68, 71, 78
57:11	50, 107, 117
58:1	79
58:4	48
58:6	48
58:10	117
58:11	79
59:1–2	60
59:3	92, 93
59:4	41
59:5	10, 40, 61
59:6	48
59:7	28
59:8	28
59:9	54, 85
59:10	72
59:11	12, 27, 52
59:13	10, 42
59:14	48
59:16	54, 72, 85
59:17	54, 85
60:1	4
60:5	59, 95, 97
60:7	54
60:9	28
60:10	4, 39
60:11	59
61:1–4	50
61:1	2, 93
61:2	50, 51, 53, 87
61:3	47, 51
61:4	47, 51, 105, 106
61:5–8	50
61:5	9, 51
61:6	35
61:7	33, 71, 78
61:8	9, 51
62:1	60
62:2	53, 54, 55, 60
62:3	3
62:4	111
62:6	53, 54, 55, 60
62:7	47, 53
62:8	47, 85
62:10	85
62:11–12a	1
62:12	12
63:1c	4
63:2	107
63:3–4	4
63:3	71
63:4	9, 117
63:5	113
63:7	105
63:7b	49
63:8	49, 97
63:8b	49
63:9–10	35
63:11	33, 35, 117
64:1	2, 93
64:2	100
64:5	28
64:9	21, 25
64:10	47, 113, 117
65:1–3	70
65:1	41
65:3	88
65:4	70, 88, 104
65:5–8	70
65:5	19
65:6	24, 25, 26
65:8	21
65:9–13	24, 70

Scripture Index

Psalms (cont.)

65:10	111
65:11	39, 71
65:13	86
66:2	9, 107
66:3–4	17
66:3	18, 19, 25
66:4	3, 9, 42
66:5–6	18
66:5	19, 26, 116
66:6	26
66:7	26, 42, 73, 92
66:8	118
66:10	80
66:11–12	80
66:11	54
66:12	80
66:13–15	108
66:13	103, 104
66:18	12
66:20	112
67:1	61, 99, 111
67:2	60
67:3	116, 118
67:4	79, 81, 87, 117, 118
67:5	116, 118
67:6	111
67:7	21, 111
68:4	3, 8, 9
68:5	39, 54, 62
68:8	10
68:10	71
68:12	33, 34, 40
68:14	12, 33, 34
68:19	12, 60, 112
68:20	12
68:23	48
68:24–26	2–3
68:24	33, 34, 36
68:25	118
68:29	33, 34, 104
68:30	118
68:32	3, 12
68:34	85
68:35	10, 17, 19, 27, 104, 112
69:3	63, 95
69:6	10, 12, 40, 63
69:9	14, 104
69:12–13	77
69:13	95, 114
69:13b	72
69:16	61, 70, 72, 95
69:17	95, 100
69:18	60, 61
69:24	40
69:28	88
69:29	60
69:30	9, 113, 116
69:32	66
69:34	113
69:35	41
69:36	9
70:4	60, 66, 116, 117
70:5	53, 58
71	47
71:1	47
71:2	58, 77, 93
71:3	53, 54
71:4	58
71:5	12
71:6	1
71:7	47
71:8	13
71:12	89
71:15	25, 60, 77
71:16	12, 25, 77
71:18	1, 25, 97
71:19	28, 69, 77
71:20	1
71:21	68
71:22	11, 78, 113, 115, 118
71:24	77
72:1	33, 34, 35, 77
72:2	79
72:3	77
72:4	59, 79
72:10	33, 34
72:11	33, 34
72:12	60
72:13–14	92
72:13	59
72:14	60
72:15	2, 111
72:17	8, 111
72:18–19	6
72:18	10, 26, 112
72:19	8, 73, 107, 112
72:20	6
73:1	70
73:11	11
73:17	104
73:20	41
73:21	94
73:23	86
73:24	1, 54, 87
73:25	28, 54, 71, 114
73:26	13, 54
73:28	12, 47, 70
74:1	4, 85, 86
74:2	14, 41, 60
74:7	104
74:9	3, 4
74:10	3, 9
74:11	97
74:12	33, 34, 36, 60
74:18	9
74:21	9, 113
74:22	40
75:1	9, 87, 115
75:2	79, 81
75:4	62
75:5	62
75:6–7	117
75:7–8	79
75:8	97
75:9	10
75:10	62
76:1	8, 68

Psalms (cont.)

Reference	Pages
76:2	41
76:3	51, 52
76:4	13
76:6	10
76:7	18, 19, 28, 93
76:8	44
76:9	59
76:10	115
76:11	18
76:12	19, 33, 34
77:1	62
77:2	12
77:3	50
77:7	4, 113
77:9	62
77:10	11, 97
77:11	26
77:13	28, 69
77:14	26, 118
77:15	10, 60, 98
77:19	98
77:20	84, 86, 87
78:4–5	26
78:5	10
78:10	73
78:11–12	26
78:12	26
78:14	13, 87
78:15	54
78:16	53
78:17	11
78:20	54
78:21	10
78:22	85
78:32	26
78:35	11, 53, 60
78:37	73
78:38	41, 62, 88
78:41–42	11
78:42	97
78:49	42
78:51–53	84
78:52	86
78:53	87
78:54	97
78:55	14
78:56	11
78:60	104, 105
78:61	13
78:62	14
78:63	113
78:65	12, 41
78:66	53
78:68	41
78:69	104
78:70–72	84
78:70	42
78:71	10, 14
78:72	87
79:1	14, 104
79:4–5a	3
79:6	9
79:7	10
79:8	61, 95
79:9	9, 60, 88, 107
79:11	69, 97
79:12–13	115
79:12	12
79:13	73, 85, 86
80:1	84, 86, 98, 105, 106
80:2	26, 41
80:2b	80
80:3	99
80:4	3, 40
80:7	40, 99
80:10	106
80:14	40, 44, 92
80:15	97
80:17	97
80:18	9
80:19	40, 99
81:1	10, 85
81:2	118
81:3	118
81:4	10
81:7	80
81:8	2, 93
81:9	42
81:16	54
82:1	79
82:2	79
82:3	39, 79
82:4	58
82:6	11
82:8	40, 79
83:1	95
83:4	8
83:5	72
83:8	97
83:16	9
83:18	8, 11, 21
84:1	40, 104
84:2	13
84:3	33, 34, 36, 40, 106
84:4	104
84:7	41
84:8	2, 10, 40, 93
84:9	38, 51, 52, 92
84:10	104
84:11	52, 71
84:12	40
84:13	85
85:1	10, 113
85:2	88
85:4	86
85:6	117
85:9–12	78
85:9	87, 107
85:11	44, 93
85:12	71
86:1	2, 93, 95
86:2	62, 85
86:3	12, 61
86:4	117
86:5	12, 70, 71, 88
86:6	2
86:7	95
86:8–9	25
86:8	77

Scripture Index

Psalms (cont.)

86:9	8, 9, 12, 42	89:18	11, 13, 33, 35, 51, 52	92:1	9, 11, 70, 115
86:10	69	89:19	117	92:2	72, 78
86:11	9, 21, 78	89:21	97, 98	92:3	118
86:12–13	68–69, 115	89:24	9, 62, 71, 78, 87, 117	92:4–5	25
86:12	9, 12			92:4	96, 115, 116
86:13	60, 71	89:25	97	92:8	73
86:14	89	89:26	34, 53, 60, 62	92:10	62, 117
86:15	12, 62, 71, 78, 94	89:27	33, 34	92:12–13	104
		89:28	34, 63, 71	92:13	104
86:16	61	89:29	34, 38	92:15	53, 80
86:17	4, 71	89:33	71, 79, 87	93	20
87:2	10, 41	89:34–35	73	93:1	25, 41, 55
87:3	41	89:36	38	93:2	38, 41, 73
87:5	11, 41	89:38	4, 38	93:4	13, 116
87:6	118	89:39	39	93:5	103, 104
88:1	60	89:44	38	94:1–2	106
88:2	93	89:46	3, 100	94:1	106
88:4	89	89:48	29	94:2	79
88:5	97	89:49	12, 71, 79	94:3	3
88:10	26	89:50–51	118	94:5	14
88:11	79	89:51	38	94:6	39
88:12	26, 77	89:52	6, 73, 112	94:7	10
88:14	4, 100	90:1	2, 12	94:9	92, 93
89:1	2, 72, 79	90:2	73	94:14	14
89:2	71, 73, 78	90:3–12	25	94:16	29
89:3–4	38, 73	90:11a	28	94:17	29
89:3	42	90:13	3	94:18	55
89:5	26, 78, 115	90:14	72, 116	94:20	39
89:6–7	18, 28	90:17	6	94:22	47, 53, 54
89:7	19	91	47	95–99	20
89:8	12, 28, 40, 77, 78	91:1	11, 12, 105	95:1	54, 116
		91:2	47, 54, 85	95:2	116
89:9–10	24	91:4	47, 52, 78, 105	95:3–5	69
89:9	42	91:5–6	21	95:3	33, 34, 36, 69
89:10	98	91:7	97	95:4–5	36, 96
89:11–12	25	91:9–12	42	95:5	24
89:11	24	91:9–10	11, 54	95:6	42, 43
89:12	9	91:9	11, 47, 54	95:7	84, 85, 86, 97
89:13	25, 97, 117	91:11	62	95:9	80
89:14	38, 72, 78	91:12	117	96:1	2
89:15	13, 99	91:14	9, 58	96:2	9, 60
89:16	9, 77	91:15	87	96:3	107, 118
89:17	62, 114, 117	91:16	60	96:4	18, 19, 68, 113

Psalms (cont.)

96:5	44
96:6	13, 104
96:7	107, 118
96:8	9, 107
96:9	42
96:10-11	116
96:10	25, 41, 55, 79, 81, 118
96:13	78, 79, 118
97:1	41, 116
97:2	38
97:6	107, 118
97:7	42, 113
97:8	41
97:9	11, 21
97:10	60, 62
97:11	13
97:12	8, 9, 115
98:1	2, 59, 97, 98
98:2-3	60
98:2	1, 77
98:3	71, 78
98:6	33, 34, 36, 118
98:9	79, 81, 118
99:1	41, 98, 105, 118
99:2-3	118
99:2	41, 69
99:3	8, 18, 19, 68, 115
99:4	10, 33, 34, 36, 76, 81
99:5	42, 98, 117
99:6	9
99:8	88
99:9	117
100:3	85, 86
100:4-5	115, 116
100:4	9, 116
100:5	70, 71, 73, 78
101:1	3, 72
101:2	3
101:6	92
101:7-8	38
101:8	41
102:1	2, 50, 93
102:2	93, 95, 100
102:5	49
102:11	105
102:12	8, 73
102:13	41, 61, 62
102:14	61
102:15	9, 21, 33, 34, 107
102:16	41, 107
102:19	44
102:20	93
102:21	9, 41
102:22	118
102:25	25, 44, 96
102:28	42
103:1	9
103:3-4	61
103:3	88
103:4	39, 60
103:5	71
103:6	76
103:8	62, 71, 94
103:11	71
103:12	89
103:13	62
103:17-18	73
103:17	71, 73, 77
103:19	38, 41, 42, 44
103:20-21	40
103:20	42
103:21	114
103:22	25, 41
104:2	13, 44
104:3-4	25
104:5	25, 55
104:13-15	24-25
104:13	25
104:15	99
104:18	47, 53
104:19a	25
104:19b	25
104:20-21	25
104:21	48
104:22-23	25
104:24-26	24
104:24	24, 25, 96
104:25	24, 68
104:27-30	25
104:27	96
104:28	24, 71, 96
104:29	96, 100
104:30	96
104:31-32	25
104:31	107
104:33	3, 113
105:1	9, 114, 118
105:2	3
105:3	9, 66, 117
105:4	65, 66, 99
105:5	94
105:6	10, 42
105:8-10	11, 73
105:9	10, 11
105:10	10
105:11	14
105:14	33, 34
105:15	38
105:20	33, 42
105:21	42
105:23	10
105:26	42
105:30	33
105:41	54
105:42	10, 42
106:1	70, 71, 73, 115
106:2	25, 29
106:3	76
106:4	60, 113-114
106:5	14, 71
106:7	26
106:8-9	26
106:8	9, 59
106:10-11	59
106:10	60

Psalms (cont.)		108:12	59	113:7–9	29, 112
106:13	25, 95	108:29	73	113:7	117
106:19	42	109:1–3	95	114:1	10
106:21	59, 69	109:5	71	114:2	41
106:22	18, 19, 26	109:12	61	114:7	9, 10
106:26	97, 117	109:13	8, 88	114:8	54
106:30	2	109:14	88	115:1	9, 72, 78, 107
106:31	76	109:17	114	115:3	44, 114
106:40	14	109:21	9, 12, 70, 72	115:4	96
106:41	42	109:23	105	115:5	92, 94
106:44	93	109:26	59, 72	115:6	93, 94
106:46	62	109:27	97	115:7	95, 96
106:47	9, 59, 115	109:28	111	115:8	85
106:48	6, 10, 73, 112	109:30–31	115	115:9	52, 53, 85
		109:30	113	115:10	52, 53, 85
107:1	70, 71, 73, 115	110:1	98	115:11	52, 53, 85
107:2	60	110:2	39, 41	115:12	111
107:5	50	110:5	12, 33, 34	115:13	68, 111
107:8	72, 115	110:6	79	115:15	44, 111
107:9	71	111:1–2	114	115:18	113
107:11	11	111:2	25, 69	116:2	93
107:13	59	111:3	73, 77	116:4	9
107:15	72, 115	111:4	62	116:5	62, 76
107:19	59	111:6–9	18	116:6	62
107:21	72, 115	111:6	14, 25, 26	116:8–9	13
107:22	25, 116	111:7	25, 77, 96	116:9	13
107:24	25	111:8	73, 78, 80	116:13	9, 60
107:30	87	111:9	8, 9, 19	116:15	92
107:31	72, 115	111:10	73	116:17	9, 116
107:32	113, 117	112:1	114	116:19	104
107:38	111	112:2	111	117:1	113
107:41	86, 117	112:3	76	117:2	71, 73, 78
107:43	29, 72	112:4	13, 62	118	47
108:1	3, 73	112:5	61	118:1–4	71
108:2	73, 118	112:6	55	118:1	70, 115
108:3–4	115	112:7	21, 85	118:6	21
108:3	40, 73, 118	112:9	62, 76, 117	118:8	47, 85
108:4	44, 68, 71, 73, 78	113:1	9, 42	118:9	47, 85
		113:2	9, 73, 111, 112, 113	118:10	9
108:5	44, 107, 117			118:11	9
108:6	59, 95, 97	113:3	9, 113	118:12	9
108:8	54	113:4	44, 107, 117	118:14	60, 85
108:10	28	113:5–6	29	118:15	27, 60, 97
108:11	4, 39	113:6	44	118:16	27, 97, 117

Psalms (cont.)		119:68	70	119:159	72, 92, 93
118:17	25	119:69	89	119:160	73, 78
118:19	115	119:72	94–95	119:164	113
118:21	60, 95, 115	119:73	96	119:166	60
118:24	117	119:74	63	119:173	97
118:25	59	119:75	78	119:174	60
118:26	9, 104, 111	119:76	72	119:175	113
118:27	62, 99, 106	119:77	62	120–134	2
118:28	115, 117	119:78	89	121:1	53
118:29	70, 71, 115	119:81	60, 63	121:2	24, 44, 53
119:2	66	119:82	3	121:3	62
119:7	115	119:84	3	121:4	41, 62
119:10	66	119:85	89	121:5	62, 106
119:12	112	119:86	79	121:7	53, 62
119:13	94	119:88	72, 95	121:8	62
119:18	26, 92	119:89–91	24	122:1	103, 104, 117
119:19	100	119:89	44, 73	122:4	9, 115
119:21	89	119:90	78	122:5	39
119:25	49	119:94	66	122:9	71, 104
119:27	26	119:105	13	123:1	44
119:29	61	119:108	113	123:2	61
119:30	61, 79	119:114	52, 63	123:3	61
119:31	49	119:120	21	124:6	112
119:35	114	119:122	71, 89	124:7–8	53
119:37	92	119:123	4	124:8	9, 24, 44, 53
119:39	70	119:124–125	42	125:1	41, 55, 85
119:40	77	119:124	72	125:2	73
119:41	59	119:129	26	125:3	39
119:42	77, 85, 95	119:132	9, 61	126:1	41
119:43	63, 78	119:135	99	126:2	86
119:44	62	119:136	61	126:3	86
119:45	66	119:137	76, 80	127:1	62
119:46	33, 34	119:138	79	127:3	14
119:48	117	119:142	73, 77	128:2	71
119:49	63	119:144	73	128:4–5	111
119:51	89	119:147	63	128:5	41, 70
119:55	9	119:148	95	129:4	76
119:57	13, 61	119:149	2, 72, 93	129:5	41
119:58	61, 99	119:151	77, 87	129:8	9, 111, 114
119:60	61	119:152	73	130:1	63
119:62	61, 115	119:153–154	60	130:2	2, 12, 93
119:64	71	119:153	92, 93	130:3	12, 29
119:65	71	119:155	66	130:4	21, 29, 86, 88
119:66	70	119:156	62	130:5	63

Scripture Index

Psalms (cont.)		136:3	12, 115	140:4	62
130:7	63, 71, 86	136:4	26, 69	140:7	12, 60
131:1	68	136:5	24, 44	140:12–13	115
131:3	63	136:7	13, 68	140:13	9
132:2	10	136:8–9	41	141:2	106, 117
132:5	10, 104	136:12	97, 98	141:6	53, 79
132:7	42, 98, 104	136:17–20	34	141:8	12, 47, 92
132:8	40, 105	136:17	33, 68	141:9	62
132:10–12	38	136:18	13, 33	142:1	2, 61
132:10	38, 42	136:19	33	142:3	50
132:11–12	38, 73	136:20	33	142:4	92
132:11	78	136:21	14	142:5	13, 47
132:13	41	136:22	14, 42	142:6	60
132:15	111	136:26	44	142:7	9, 115
132:17	38, 62	136:36	115	143:1	2, 77, 78, 93, 95
132:18	39	137:1	41		
133:1	114	137:3	41	143:4	50
133:3	41, 114	137:4	2	143:5	25, 96
134:1	42, 104	137:6	49	143:7	95, 100
134:2	117	137:9	53	143:8	71, 85, 117
134:3	24, 41, 44, 111	138:1	113, 115	143:9	60
135:1	9, 113	138:2	9, 42, 72, 78, 104, 115	143:10	70, 81, 87, 96, 114
135:2	104				
135:3	6, 9, 70	138:4–5	69	143:11	9, 77
135:4	10, 14	138:4	33, 34, 94, 115	143:12a	72
135:5	12, 69	138:5	107	144:1	53, 97, 112
135:6	114	138:6	117	144:2	47, 51, 52, 54, 58
135:7	25	138:7	59, 97		
135:10–11	34	138:8	25, 71, 73, 96	144:4	105
135:10	26, 33	139:7	96	144:7	60, 97
135:11–12	27	139:8	44	144:9	2, 3, 113, 118
135:11	33, 34	139:10	87, 97	144:10	33, 35, 42, 59
135:12	14	139:11	13		
135:13	8, 73	139:13	94	144:11	51, 60
135:14	42, 79	139:14	19, 25, 26, 115	144:12	104
135:15	96			144:13	86
135:16–17	94	139:16	92	145:1	9, 33, 34, 36, 117
135:16	92	139:17	6		
135:17	93, 95	139:18	86	145:2	9, 113
135:18	85	139:19	9	145:3–7	19
135:21	41, 112	139:20	117	145:3	68, 69, 113
136:1–26	71, 73	139:23–24	80	145:3b	36
136:1	70, 115	139:24	87, 92, 93	145:4	25
136:2	115	140:3	48	145:5	107

Psalms (cont.)

145:6	19, 69
145:7	70, 77
145:8	62, 69, 71, 94
145:9	25, 62, 70
145:10	25, 116
145:11	25, 41, 107
145:12	25, 41, 107
145:13	41, 73
145:15–16	96
145:15	92
145:16	114
145:17	25, 76
145:18	78, 87
145:19	114
145:20	62
145:21	9
146	37
146:1	113
146:2	113
146:3	37, 59, 85
146:4	37
146:5	10, 37, 53
146:6	24, 37, 44, 63, 73, 78
146:7–9	37, 53
146:9	39, 62
146:10	37, 41, 73
147:1–6	69
147:1	6, 69, 70
147:3–5a	26
147:3	69
147:4–5	68
147:4	8, 69
147:7–11	69
147:7	69, 116
147:8–9	70
147:10	113, 114
147:11	63, 70, 71, 113
147:12–20	69
147:12	41, 69, 113
147:13	70, 111
147:15–18	25
147:17	29
147:19–20	70
147:19	10
148:1	113
148:2	40, 42, 113
148:3–5	24
148:3	13, 25, 113
148:4	113
148:5	9, 24
148:7a–8	25
148:7	113
148:8	95
148:9	113
148:10	113
148:11–12	113
148:11	33, 34, 79
148:13	9, 44
148:14	62, 87, 117
149:1	2
149:2	33, 34, 36, 41, 117
149:3	9, 113, 118
149:4	60, 113
149:4b	39
149:6	95
149:8	33, 34
150:1	113
150:2	25, 69
150:3–5	113
150:3	118
150:4	118
150:5	118
150:6	6

Proverbs

17:9	88
28:13	88

Ecclesiastes

2:8	14

Song of Songs

1:16	5
7:6	5

Isaiah

2:3	10
37:36	36
40:6–8	74
42:6	14
49:26	10
53:6	87
60:13	98
60:14	41
60:16	10
66:1	99

Jeremiah

21:12	38
50:29	11
51:5	11

Lamentations

2:1	98–99

Ezekiel

39:7	11

Joel

2:13	94

Jonah

2:7–9	108
2:7	50
2:9	51
4:2	94

Micah

4:2	10
7:19	90

Zechariah

6:10	71
9:9	43
13:7	89

Malachi

3:17	14

Scripture Index

Matthew

1:6	43
2:1	43
2:2	43
4:6	54
5:7	64
5:35	43, 99
9:8	21, 118
9:27	64
9:30	64
9:36	89, 90
10:6	90
10:16	90
10:18	43
11:23	119
15:22	64
15:24	90
15:28	64
15:31	118
17:2	100
17:5	22
17:6	22
17:15	64
17:18	64
18:10	101
18:33	64
19:4	30
20:30	64, 67
20:31	64, 67
20:34	64
21:5	43
21:10	30
21:46	22
23:37	105
25:32	89
25:34	43
25:40	43
26:31	89, 90
27:11	43
27:37	43
27:51	107
27:54	22

Mark

2:7	30
2:12	118
4:41	22, 30
5:15	21
5:19	64
6:34	89
10:47	64, 67
10:48	64
10:52	64
12:12	22
13:9	43
13:19	30
14:27	89

Luke

1:9	107
1:33	74
1:47	63
1:52	120
2:8	89
2:9	22
2:11	63
2:15	89
2:18	89
2:20	89
4:10–11	54
4:15	119
5:21	30
5:25–26	118
7:16	119
7:49	30
8:35	21
9:29	100
9:34	22
10:15	119
10:24	43
13:13	118
13:34	105
14:11	119
15	56
17:13	64
17:14	64, 109
17:15	118
18:13	67
18:14	119
18:38–39	64
18:42–43	64
18:43	119
20:19	22
20:42	119
21:12	43
22:25	43
23:47	119
24:44	119

John

1:4	14
1:49	43
2:21	107
3:14	119
3:16	55
4:24	92
4:42	63
6:19	22
6:51	74
6:58	74
7:2	14
8:12	13, 14
8:28	119
9:5	14
9:35–37	30
10	90
10:2	90
10:11	89, 90
10:12	90
10:14	89
10:15	90
10:16	90
11:4	119
11:9	14
12:13	43
12:32–34	119
12:34	30
12:36	14
14:13	119
14:16	74
17:4	119

Scripture Index

John (cont.)
19:15	43
21:25	29

Acts
1:20	119
2:33	119
4:21	119
4:25–26	43
5:31	63, 119
7:10	43
8:32	90
9:15	43
11:18	119
13:21	43
13:23	63
13:33	119
19:27	107
21:20	119
25:13	43

Romans
1:25	30, 74
6:23	88
7:25	30
8:35	30
8:36	90
9:5	74
9:15	64
9:18	64
11:30	64
11:31	64
11:32	64
11:36	74
15:9	119
16:27	74

1 Corinthians
1:8	81
1:9	81
2:12	2
3:16	108
3:17	108
6:19	108
9:13	107
9:25	74
10:13	81
11:9	30
13:12	101
14:26	119
15:42–44	55

2 Corinthians
1:18	81
3:18	101
4:1	64
4:6	100
6:16	108
6:18	14
9:13	119
11:7	119
11:31	74
11:32	43

Galatians
1:24	119
3:6–9	20

Ephesians
2:10	30
2:15	30
2:19–22	108
2:21–22	108
3:9	30
4:11	90
4:24	30
5:19	119
5:23	63
6:10–18	55
6:14	55
6:15	55
6:16	55
6:17	55
6:18	55

Philippians
2:27	64
3:20–21	64

Colossians
1:16	30
3:10	30
3:16	119

1 Thessalonians
4:17	74
5:24	81

2 Thessalonians
1:9	101
3:3	81

1 Timothy
1:1	63
1:13	64
1:15	81
1:16	64
1:17	43, 92
2:2	43
2:3	63
3:1	81
4:3	30
4:9–10	81
4:10	63
6:15	43
6:16	74, 92
6:19	55

2 Timothy
1:9b–10	64
2:11–12a	81
2:13	81

Titus
1:3	63
1:4	63
1:9	81
2:10	63
2:14	14, 63
3:4–7	63
3:8	81

Hebrews

2:17	81
3:2	81
5:6	74
6:20	74
7:1	43
7:17	74
7:21	74
7:24	74
7:28	74
10:14	74
10:23	81
11:11	81
13:8	74
13:20	89

James

4:10	119

1 Peter

1:23	74
1:25	74
2:5	108
2:9	14
2:10	64
2:13	43
2:17	43
2:25	90
4:11	119
4:16	119
4:19	81
5:6	119
5:9	55

2 Peter

1:1	63
1:11	63
2:20	63
3:2	63
3:18	63, 74

1 John

1:9	81
2:17	74
4:14	63

2 John

2	74

Jude

13	74
25	63

Revelation

1:5	43, 81
1:8	14, 15
3:12	108
3:14	81
4:8	14, 15
4:11	30
5:2	30
5:5	30
5:9	119
6:15–17	43
6:16	101
10:6	30
11:17	14, 14
14:3	119
15:3	14, 15, 43, 119
16:7	14, 15
16:14	14, 15
17:14	43
18:13	90
19:6	14, 15
19:11	81
19:15	14, 15
19:16	43
19:17–21	43
21:3	108
21:5	81
21:22	14, 15, 108
22:3–4	101
22:6	81

www.ingramcontent.com/pod-product-compliance
Lightning Source LLC
Chambersburg PA
CBHW071501160426
43195CB00013B/2179